PERMISSION TO MATTER

Permission to Matter takes women seriously, and Bekah Stewart doesn't waste a single page. This book is a masterclass in feminine spirituality, and the church will be far better for its existence.

— SHANNON K. EVANS, Author of *The Mystics Would Like a Word* and *Rewilding Motherhood*

Bekah Stewart has written a book for me—a tender, readable guide to reclaiming the uniquely female spirituality, agency, vocation, and authority offered by Our Mother God in the Bible. This book is not about taking down the church patriarchy; it is about empowering women to live fully awake and fully human. I have been waiting for this book for my whole life.

— LIZ CHARLOTTE GRANT, Author of *Knock at the Sky: Seeking God in Genesis after Losing Faith in the Bible*

In this soulful and practical book that touches on the deep and vulnerable experiences of so many women of faith, Bekah Stewart is a wise guide, offering a path to greater healing, freedom, and empowerment that is so needed in our culture. Through honest reflections, contemplative exercises, and guiding questions to practice in our real lives, Permission to Matter offers just that— permission and challenge to listen to the longing in our souls to stand up, wake up, and live boldly, together.

— KATHY ESCOBAR, Co-Founder of The Refuge and Author of *Practicing: Changing Yourself to Change the World*

Permission to Matter is about more than the reclamation of women's spirituality and value, although if it were only that it would be an incredible and liberating guide for the feminine spiritual journey. Permission to Matter is about the full relational empowerment of our beloved humanity made in the image of the Triune

God. Bekah Stewart's sharp wit and clear wisdom lead us toward a fuller Gospel, one that will make us all whole.

— TARA OWENS, CSD, CSDS, Spiritual Director, Supervisor and Executive Director of Anam Cara Ministries, Author of *Embracing the Body: Finding God in Our Flesh & Bone*

PERMISSION TO MATTER

**RECLAIMING WOMEN'S HUMANITY AND
AUTHORITY AT THE INVITATION OF JESUS**

BEKAH STEWART

**PUNCHLINE
PUBLISHERS**
Franklin, TN

First Paperback Edition June 2025

Cover Design and Interior Design by Erica Krysl

Artwork by Shannon Thomas

ISBN 978-1-955051-43-9 (Paperback)

ISBN 978-1-955051-44-6 (eBook)

Library of Congress Control Number: 2025911140

Published in association with Punchline Publishers

www.punchlineagency.com

www.BekahStewart.com

@BekahStewart

For my favorite girl in the whole world.
You know who you are.

And for the Mercy Tuckers and Kristin Wrights of the world.
Women who see us, believe us, trust our deep embodied
knowing, but more importantly, trust their own.

TABLE OF CONTENTS

AUTHOR'S NOTE

On my desk, I keep a quote from Anais Nin that reads, "The role of a writer is not to say what we can all say, but what we are unable to say." This book, for me, is about saying the things that I know countless women cannot say.

How do I know what women cannot say? Because I have sat with hundreds of women over the years, heard their stories, and companioned their pain. I know this because *I have been the woman with plenty she cannot say.*

I am a spiritual director, vocational coach, and former pastor.[1] Every year, I lead groups of women through the content found in these pages, and every year I am astounded by the enormity of each woman's life, living just below the surface.

To be a woman—by design—is to be a powerhouse of deep knowing. We have been given everything needed to live in fullness and wisdom. And yet, the cultural (read: patriarchal and too often "Christian") messages continue to weigh us down and hold us back. They tell us to "Stay Asleep. Play Small. Be Invisible." In truth, these messages are antithetical to the invitation Jesus offers women in the Gospels, which, I believe, is to "Wake Up, Stand Up, and Come Out of Hiding."

Some will find fault in these pages, believing this material to be dangerous in how it asks women to take ownership of their lives. *They're right.* Much of what I have to say will make those who are satisfied with the current state of church and Christian female development very uncomfortable.

Some will find fault here, believing this material to be too binary in how it addresses a person's gender and sex. *They're also right.* I'm choosing to speak specifically to and for those who identify as women and by contrasting male and female spirituality. Even within this particular audience, I'm aware at times, there will be limits and generalizations. I know that I (a white, able-bodied, heterosexual, cisgender, middle-class, married mother) will not and cannot represent every woman.[2]

There's one more thing you should know about me. When it comes to Christian culture, I don't have much to lose. I've been uninvited to conservative spaces on account of saying yes to leadership in a progressive church, and uninvited to progressive spaces on account of not being grateful enough for what that space provided me as a woman.

I unabashedly, unapologetically, and unswervingly want more. I want more for me. I want more for you. I want more for the Church. The Church will never truly be good news for women if women aren't truly good news for the Church.

INTRODUCTION

PERMISSION TO MATTER

There is no place so awake and alive as the edge of becoming. But more than that, birthing the kind of woman who can authentically say, 'My soul is my own,' and then embody it in her life, her spirituality, and her community is worth the risk and hardship.

— Sue Monk Kidd[3]

IN college, a guy asked my dad for permission to date me. That's right—I said date, not marry. This ought to offer you some insight into the fairly conservative and Christian context I found myself in at the time. Luckily, I have a father who was as weirded out by this as I was, and let the guy know I was fully capable of making that decision on my own.

It was in that same conservative, Christian context where I watched female mentors brought up on a platform at events. The primary male leader would hand over the microphone, but not before giving a thorough explanation as to why he was granting them permission to speak to a mixed-gender audience. Apparently, a woman couldn't be trusted to speak, lead, or date without permission.

If you've grown up in Christian spaces, you know that in the world of female-permission giving, these stories are mild at best. I'm grateful to say I did not grow up in an extreme fundamentalist family. Regardless, I still had plenty of opportunities to be shaped by a culture that clearly defined where permission came from: *outside of me.*

Permission is about power and points to what one is allowed to do. When we are children, it's appropriate to have permission given and restricted by an external source. How late to stay out, what words to say, who we spend our time with. We need healthy and aware authority figures in our lives to protect and direct us as we develop. But to be human is to grow up. Children become adults, and learn to give themselves their own permissions. *Or do they?*

Have you ever noticed how impossibly difficult it is for some women to shake the "good little girl" mentality? All of a sudden we are 32 years old and navigating the world as a grown-ass woman, but have never fully transitioned into adults. We wait for someone to rescue us, assume others know better, and continue to modify our behavior (and our bodies) to fit the culturally acceptable norms. We allow our permission to remain in the hands of others, functioning as if our authority comes from somewhere external. Like daughters to a cultural father, we remain good little girls.[4]

Fortunately, life has a way of offering waking moments when we are forced to glance at the book cover of our life, and see that in place of our name as the author, Peter Patriarchy has been writing the story all along.[5]

For years, I worked for a fairly conservative Christian non-profit. In many ways, it was an important time in my life that grew me, and deepened my love for Jesus and others, but it mostly reaffirmed the same permission-giving paradigms I had always been given—paradigms that relied on me staying asleep. When I stepped into leadership at a more progressive, post-evangelical church, I was ripe for waking up. This faith community was one that pushed the boundaries, fearlessly exploring the goodness and expansiveness of God.

During my first two years serving as an elder, we walked through a season of discernment, asking ourselves, "Will we open our tables wider to fully include our LGBTQIA+ brothers and sisters?" I was in my 30s and, for the first time, was asked to reconsider ways in which I had viewed God, the Bible, and the world. It was one of the most anxiety-producing and beautiful experiences of my life. It shook me, knocking the evangelical, little-girl-sized-socks right off my feet. No one was going to give me the answers or tell me exactly what to do. Instead, I was being asked to tap into my own decision-making abilities. It forced me to find my voice, and locate my God-given authority and agency . . . *in me.*

Those two years invited me into a new and expansive way of seeing our LGBTQIA+ community, *and* they invited me into a new and expansive way of seeing myself. I was waking up to deeply engrained patterns of outsourcing my permission and dismissing my own intuitive knowing. To be sure, it was an empowering and defining experience in my story, but I wouldn't exactly describe it as liberating in the way you might expect.

Before I could begin to be set free and reclaim my own permission, something that had been shut off in me needed to be released. A deep sorrow rose up in me, and a seemingly never-ending stream of tears flowed out. It's like I tapped into a previously unplumbed source of grief that had existed in me all my life, passed down among women over thousands of years. Instead of initially feeling confident and strong in my new realizations, I felt overwhelmingly sad. My body was telling me something about the collective wound we hold as women.

Our bodies are so wise. According to Scripture, a woman's body is a temple—a dwelling place of God—which is to say, a dwelling place of Authority (1 Cor. 6:19). She is a powerhouse of deep knowing. But for most of us, she has experienced a lifetime of neglect. We have not honored and respected her. We have not trusted and listened to her. We have shamed and treated her with contempt, or just dismissed her altogether. Mostly, we just didn't know she mattered.

To survive in a world that tells us we are unacceptable from the beginning, we drift off to dreamland in order to survive. Only parts of us are allowed to show themselves in broad daylight—those deemed culturally appropriate—and over time, we come to see and shape our lives around those parts. The rest are forgotten and seemingly left for dead. But here's the good news: *they aren't dead*, just asleep.

Waking moments are like little invitations to wake back up to our full humanity. It's as if God whispers in our ears, "You matter more than you've been led to believe." This knowledge is initially startling, and because we have been taught that our own inner-knowing is not trustworthy, we resist it. To complicate matters further, waking moments tend to be unpleasant, often accompanied by angst, and extremely disruptive—not exactly conducive for the good little girl version of ourselves.

Herein lies our dilemma:

Will we step into adulthood and into our full humanity, even if it inevitably rubs against the status quo? Doing so will stir up foreign feelings we will be tempted to push down or excuse away. It will mean choosing to keep our eyes open, staying awake, and looking honestly at the patriarchal reality that becomes increasingly and painfully clear. It will require growing up, which means no more "good little girl."

I've been a woman in a man's world for long enough to know how this book will rub some who read it. I'm not going to try and downplay the fact that this will be disruptive. Stepping fully into who God created you to be will inevitably agitate and unsettle your world. It has the potential to ruin your life . . . in the best possible ways.

What I offer here is one possible archetype or pattern for the female spiritual journey. It's not the only path, nor should it be, but perhaps it is a place where you, my friend, will find yourself, like I have found me. In the pages that follow, we will explore Jesus' invitation to Wake Up, Stand Up, and Come Out of Hiding. Responding to this will mean relocating our permission within. And so, you must decide: Will you allow yourself to see that permission is *already* yours, and take back what you have given away? The pen is in your hand, as securely as your God-given authority and agency runs through your veins. It's time to write your own permission slips, and story.

If there's going to be a book written about your life, make sure it's *your* name on the cover.

Before we jump in, I'd encourage you to grab a journal and pen. There is plenty of information to collect in these pages, but information does not automatically equal transformation. I believe this book can guide you into some deep inner (and outer) work if you will allow it to. In the chapters ahead, I invite you to personalize the material. In each chapter, you will find questions, prompts, and exercises for further reflection. Additionally, you will find a group discussion guide in the appendix.

CHAPTER ONE

A NEW ROAD MAP

DISCOVERING THE FEMALE SPIRITUAL JOURNEY

Women do have a quest at this time in culture...to heal the deep wound of the feminine. It is a very important inner journey toward being a fully integrated, balanced, and whole human being.

— Maureen Murdock[6]

MY earliest memory of God is the day, at 4 years old, when I watched my balloon fly up to the heavens. I had just returned from a funeral where, for the first time, I saw a dead body lying in a casket. Out on the big lawn of our home in the country, I remember staring into the sky until my balloon slowly disappeared, acknowledging that both the balloon and that dead person had somehow floated up to God—or at least that was what I was told. I didn't question it. I'm not sure I cared much about how exactly either one would eventually reach God. What mattered was that God was there waiting and that God apparently existed in the fluffy clouds. It seemed like a nice place to go, for both people and balloons.

I've always been drawn to the human experience with the Divine and curious about how the God who existed in the clouds was involved in our day-to-day lives. Of course, over time, I have come to find God in more places than just the sky. It turns out that God is as expansive as the firmament *and* as down-to-earth as the ground we walk on every day. The Bible tells us that human beings were made of some mix of big-sky-expansiveness and literal ground dirt and that this human concoction came to life as God breathed right into our freshly clay-formed nostrils (Gen. 2:7). And so, God is also in us. In the fiber of our beings. In the weaving together of our stories. In how we each make our way through the world, seeing only as we can see, knowing only what we can know. *What an incredibly intimate mystery.*

Here we are on this journey of learning to reach up, dig down, and breathe deep. It is the journey of becoming most fully human—most fully who God created us to be.

We are often taught that this journey of becoming should be like a long buffet line. I pay $19.99, grab a plate, and begin perusing the unending options of "how to live" behind the glass sneeze guard. *Oh, that persona looks good. I will take a little bit of perfection, a scoop of the pretty/pleasing combo, and a double helping of being utterly reliable in every way.* And then we hustle, hustle, hustle to scarf and keep down all that we've put on our plate. Women are astoundingly good at morphing into a million different forms that please the world around them while ignoring—and even being afraid of—our actual God-given design.

What would happen if we consciously stepped out of this buffet line and paused long enough to honestly ask: *Who am I becoming on the journey of becoming me?*

To wholeheartedly ask and confront this question is to embark on a grand adventure of coming undone—in order to become. Of releasing to take hold. Of ending to begin. We find that who we are is not discovered by going outside of ourselves, not ordering from a buffet line set out for us, but by uncovering what is within—what is *already* there.

I want to help you discover what is *already* there, but before we can do that, we first have to acknowledge the unhelpful options, or what I'll call "road maps," we've been given in the buffet line of life.

Unhelpful Road Map #1 - Your Starting Point Is Bad

As a little girl, I would lay in my bed and pray the sinner's prayer over and over. I've always been someone who likes to feel prepared, and what's more important to be prepared for than eternity? It was hard for me to imagine that those words could stick if my only propensity all the time was for evil. That might sound a little extreme, but this is exactly what many of us have been taught. The idea of original sin is popularly taught in many churches, and assumes the human starting place is bad, evil, and bent toward sin. Jesus, then, acts as a bridge covering our sinful predisposition and making us acceptable before God.

In her book, *Original Blessing*, Danielle Shroyer explains, "If our human nature separated us from God, we need more than a bridge. We need to be disembodied, which is a weird place to end up in a faith that's based on God becoming human."[7] You would think that if God chose to become human, we might have a higher view of the body. Instead, we've been taught that our human nature is bad—so unlike God—and so our flesh becomes a liability, responsible for our inevitable sin. We ignore the wisdom of our bodies and assume they are part of some temporary package that won't make it to eternity. For many of us, this disembodied tension is something we have built a life around (much to our disembodied detriment), mostly because we didn't realize there was an alternative. Do a little digging into church history and you will quickly unmask the illusion that there is one, airtight, accepted-across-time-and-space way to interpret Scripture generally, and specifically as it pertains to original sin.

Did you know that the church existed for hundreds of years before the idea of original sin was even introduced and that whole segments of the Christian church have *never* adopted it? Neither

the Nicene nor Apostle's Creed suggest it either. So, if you're starting to wonder, "Am I still considered orthodox if I accept this?"
Rest assured, you're just fine. It's not a "biblical given" that our
starting place is bad.

Original sin is a harmful belief for everyone, *but especially for
women*. Implying that we are inherently bad hands humanity
a scarce narrative, and any time you start with scarcity, you end
up with hierarchy. A deficit of any resource—even human goodness—produces competition. There isn't room for everyone to be
"on top," so systems are created to determine status. People are
then ranked based on a set of values where some are considered
superior and others inferior, and historically and in the Church,
being a woman was considered inferior. You don't need to be an
expert on history to see this. Some of our greatest Christian influences—the early Church Fathers who significantly shaped the
orthodox Christian faith passed down to us—participated in this
hierarchy by deeming women as inferior and even dangerous. In
Introducing Feminist Theology, Lisa Isherwood and Dorothea Mc-
Ewan compile some examples:

> Jerome, Ambrose, Tertullian, Clement of Alexandria, Cyril
> of Alexandria, [and] John Damascene displayed consider-
> able hostility toward women; the language they employed
> was not just culturally conditioned misogyny but vicious
> ridicule and obscene stereotype. Tertullian's dictum: "Wom-
> an, you are the devil's gateway. You have led astray one
> whom the devil would not dare attack directly. It is your
> fault that the Son of God has to die; you should always go
> in mourning and in rags . . . You destroyed so easily God's
> image, man" (Armstrong 1986: 55) and St John Chrysotom's
> words: "Among all savage beasts none is found so harmful
> as woman" (quoted by Beauvoir 1988: 129) . . . Augustine
> can only believe that the redemption of women occurs in

some secondary fashion, while Aquinas cannot understand why God created this "misbegotten male" . . . Aquinas held that women would not have been created at all had they not been required for the service of men and they were only conceived when a damp south wind was blowing (cf. Ranke-Heinemann 1990).[8]

Ironically, women pay thousands of dollars to learn from these early Church Fathers to earn seminary degrees that open up a very limited number of doors into a man's church world. (It's me. Hi. I'm the problem. It's me.)[9] When women are spoken and written about in this way, from our own Church Fathers, and without pushback, it's easy to believe this is our only path forward.

When our starting point is bad, the spiritual journey inevitably becomes one of moving away from and out of our humanity (i.e. "I am bad, and my body is bad") instead of moving toward and into our unique way of human-being. We become trapped in a scarce mentality and as a result, set out to earn what is already ours. We feel a deep and desperate need to prove something, which can lead us to give *away* ourselves rather than simply give *of* ourselves. In a patriarchal world—which is inherently scarce and hierarchical—other women become our competition. We compare ourselves to one another and compete for the limited opportunities this broken system provides. Ultimately, how we move through the world and relate to one another hinges on this basic assumption about our goodness and worth (or lack thereof).

How does the narrative change if our starting point is good? What if God calling humanity "very good" (Gen. 1:31) from the birth of creation *actually* speaks to the truest truth of our core identity? Why wouldn't it? As Danielle Shroyer points out, if "the man and the woman in the garden of Eden didn't have a sin nature but could choose to sin, isn't it possible that the same could be said for us?"[10] It seems pretty biblical to me that God's economy would be one of abundance and not scarcity. It's a very different story when instead of hustling to make up for what we lack, we are living into what God always meant for us to be in the first place.

To truly embark on the journey of becoming most fully human, one must partner with God in the lifelong dance of accepting their identity as the Beloved. Henri Nouwen described it this way: "From the moment we claim the truth of being the Beloved, we are faced with the call to become who we are. Becoming the Beloved is the great spiritual journey we have to make."[11]

This, in and of itself, is a journey of epic proportions for women: to show up in the world and confidently claim our birthright—that we are good. To know deep in our bones that we are worthy and enough and that our very existence genuinely matters—not just in supporting roles, but as the lead in our own story.

It's hard to do the work necessary to embrace who we are, uncovering and claiming what is *already there*, if we don't believe we are worthy. It's like setting up all the resources for a major archeological dig even though the whole time you don't believe there's anything there to find. No one is going to do that. And so, first things first: You are God's Beloved. You are *Very Good*. It is your starting point, and it's where your journey of becoming is meant to head.

Unhelpful Road Map #2 – Men and Women's Spiritual Journeys Follow the Same Framework

Throughout church history, many models have been offered for the spiritual life. The purpose of these frameworks is to help us make sense of the human journey with God. Examples include John of the Cross's *Dark Night of the Soul* and Teresa of Avila's *The Interior Castle*. More recently, Walter Brueggemann's work on the Psalms and his paradigm of "Orientation, Disorientation, New Orientation" and Richard Rohr's writing, especially his excellent work on male spirituality. These trusted guides (and many more) have provided us with possible road maps for the spiritual journey.

It is Rohr's work, in particular, that has had a profound impact on me. Like so many others, he has been a fresh voice in my own spiritual life, revitalizing what has felt at times like a dying and nonsensical faith. Just as I entered my thirties, Rohr published *Falling Upward: A Spirituality for the Two Halves of Life*. I was primed for a resource that could offer a framework for where I had been and where I was headed.

According to Rohr, life is made up of two halves, and each includes developmental tasks.[12] The book is stocked full of wise insights for anyone's journey and had a large influence in my circles. But, what I began to hear over and over in various contexts was Rohr's material being presented with an emphasis on a male-specific trajectory and with no caveats given for women.[13] The trajectory was described like this: In the first half of life, we ascend and build our "container," or who we are, and there comes a point in life—often in midlife—where we must come face-to-face with our limitations, surrender to a higher power, and begin a journey of descent. This descent is typically characterized by denial of the self, letting go, giving up of power, and a sense of coming down the ladder.

Now, I don't mean to imply that there is nothing for me to glean from this wisdom, but it has always rubbed me a bit. It's as if someone has given me a really nice sweater that is two sizes too small. I've managed to get it on, but let's be honest—it doesn't fit. Certainly, confronting limits, surrendering to a higher power, and embarking on a journey of descent is a powerful and very necessary path *for men* in a patriarchal world. But, I'm a woman in patriarchy. Is the journey into full humanity for me as a woman that of descent? *Isn't that what I've been doing this whole time?*

I have often been left wanting when it comes to finding myself in stories and models that were made by men for men—where men are central, set against the backdrop of an apparently male God. As Mary Daly famously wrote, "If God is male, then male is God."[14] Just as we have defaulted to reading "women" and "she/her" into the "he/him," "mankind," and "brotherhood" of the Bible, we have also read women into the traditional male spirituality frameworks, even ones created by very well-intended and wise men along the way. And for the record, even Richard Rohr suggests that the path for women is not actually one of descent, but instead a movement upward (see footnote 13). But, for some (patriarchal?) reason, this caveat is never publicly referenced, and women continue to be offered a one-size-fits-all path.

As a result, women are typically left with two options: to play a supporting role in the male journey, or to attempt to plug our female self into a male journey model that doesn't completely fit; stand alongside to cheer him on, or become just like him. I'm not a fan of either. Women are too often limited to dreaming within these confines, but what of being a woman in *God's world* (not man's)? God, who is neither male nor female, and yet contains the fullness of both masculine and feminine?

Unhelpful Road Map #3 - Men and Women Struggle with the Same Sin

It wasn't until I came across the work of Carol Lakey Hess that I began to clarify what my dissonance with male spirituality models was really about. In her book, *Caretakers of our Common House: Women's Development in Communities of Faith,* Hess points out that because our theology over time has been mostly male-written and informed, it has overemphasized the sins of pride and self-centeredness.[15] Hess argues that, although these are the appropriate sins for a man in a patriarchal world to contend with, they miss the mark when it comes to the female journey. Instead, for a woman, the primary sin that must be contended with is that of *self-abnegation*—a big word that is worth breaking down.

Self refers to a person's essential being that differentiates them from others, and *negation* is the denial of something. Self-abnegation, then, refers to the act of rejecting or renouncing the self.

When you combine an overemphasis on pride, and a general disregard of the unique female journey, what you end up with is extremely problematic for women. Hess explains, "When sin as pride is generalized, self-abnegation is rendered a virtue and harmfully reinforced."[16] In other words, when it is assumed that pride is everyone's primary issue, we begin to treat the act of self-abnegation—rejecting the self—as a kind of universal virtue or value. We praise it, fan its flame, and affirm those who practice it. In turn, we critique, attempt to squash, and label those who don't. Instead of encouraging women to act in ways that will counter their tendency to reject or renounce the self, *we harmfully reinforce it.*

Out of a desire to faithfully follow Jesus, I had accepted the *male* path—hook, line, and sinker. I fully heeded warnings about pride and believed there was always more of myself to give away. I learned to live a life where the very invitation I needed to move into my full humanity was understood as sin and to be avoided at all costs, while the very thing I needed to reject and avoid I counted as a virtue. The only outcome for a woman in this predicament is to become a walking apology, which is what I became.

A walking apology lives primarily small. She is astoundingly aware of her surroundings and is careful not to take up space, or rub up against culturally conditioned boundaries. She learns to say what she needs to say with a kind of temperance. Her strength is channeled into astounding restraint. She suppresses big feelings like anger, believing them to be inappropriate for a woman to display. She learns to live a life where male is the default and pleasantly weaves her way around it.

How could she question the Bible? How could she question Male-God? There is an order to life, designed by Male God, and so she faithfully keeps her head down and continues walking—*apologetically*—forward. Clarissa Pinkola Estés puts it this way:

> When a woman is exhorted to be compliant, cooperative, and quiet, to not make upset or go against the old guard, she is pressed into living a most unnatural life—a life that is self-binding . . . without innovation. The worldwide issue for women is that under such conditions they are not only silenced, they are put to sleep. Their concerns, their viewpoints, their own truths vaporized.[17]

In reality, a walking apology is sleepwalking, because to sustain denying her humanity like this, one must fall asleep.

This is not to say that women will never struggle with pride, or that men will never struggle with self-rejection. It is, however, bringing light to that which impedes a woman's journey into her full humanity. It will serve us to pay attention, and to begin to ask the question: how does a woman wake up to the fullness of her life? Offering her a male-specific road map is not the answer.

Unhelpful Road Map #4: Men Be Superhuman, Women Be Subhuman

Steve Cuss, author of *Managing Leadership Anxiety: Yours and Theirs*, has coined this clever phrase: "exactly human-sized." In his context, he is speaking to our relationship with anxiety and our tendency to try and be God-sized, or take on more than is humanly possible. The invitation, then, is to be exactly human-sized, releasing what is God's to God, and owning what is appropriately ours. Being exactly human-sized is similar to what I mean when speaking of becoming fully human, but I would add a dimension to Cuss's description. In addition to trying to be God-sized, or attempting to be more than human-sized, it is also possible to attempt to become smaller, or something *less than* human-sized, and it comes as a result of self-abnegation. We have something to say, but we hold back. We see injustice, but we are too afraid to name it. We have the power to do good, but we resist. We have a particular skill or gift to offer, but we stay hidden.

In a patriarchal world, I would argue that while men are generally given the message: "You must be more than you actually are," women are given the message: "You must be less than you actually are."[18] Both of these messages are harmful, because both resist our full humanity, or being *exactly human-sized*.

For example, a man may be tempted to pursue and misuse power, while a woman may give up her prophetic voice and responsibilities. Both lead to unjust and unhealthy realities. Eventually, both men and women must face how these inhuman messages and their trajectories are harmful, and decide how they will respond.

The male and female spiritual journeys have the same ultimate goal: full humanity, or becoming exactly human-sized. But how we will get there, and what is necessary in moving into full humanity will be different. Generally speaking, because men have been told that they are to become more than human-sized, their journey must include descent, and they must contend with the sin of pride (as suggested by Carol Lakey Hess). Because women have been told to become less than human-sized, their journey must include ascent and they must contend with the sin of self-abnegation.

For a woman, the invitation is not down, but up.

By "up," I'm not implying some kind of unhealthy power trip or even a reversal of the current reality where suddenly women are more than human and men are less. This would only

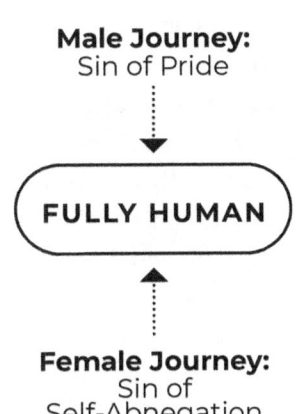

Male Journey:
Sin of Pride

↓

FULLY HUMAN

↑

Female Journey:
Sin of
Self-Abnegation

land us in the same unhealthy pickle with a different female-specific flavor. No, the goal is not getting anyone or everyone to "the top." The goal is alignment with our full humanity—where both men and women faithfully own and steward who God has created them to be.

I realize this model might feel binary and oversimplified, and there is some truth to that. When we add the layers of race, ethnicity, sexual orientation, socio-economic status, etc., these lines can be blurred, or more likely, levels are added. Power and privilege will impact a person's starting point and the pace at which they ascend or descend. Regardless, the point remains: the spiritual journey is about becoming most fully human, and we must examine our trajectory and honestly assess if the path we are walking is making us more than, less than, or exactly human-sized.

A New Roadmap: Up, Up, and Awake

For a woman, the spiritual journey up must include a reclamation. The self she has denied, rejected, and hidden away must be reclaimed and then unleashed to truly and fully live. As empowering as this may sound, it will come at a cost and will be accompanied by grief. This reclamation will require an acknowledgment that she has, in fact, already been on the male second half of life journey.

Here's what I mean: To be a girl—in a patriarchal culture of any kind—is to be seen, treated as, and asked to accept her identity as *inherently limited*. It becomes the water she swims in; the air she breathes. She remains mostly unconscious to this reality but instinctively knows that to "survive" and to remain acceptable, she must 1) confront her "limits," 2) surrender to a higher power (patriarchy), and 3) embark on a journey of descent, putting desires and hopes secondary to being small, humble, and quiet. In light of this, a woman's task on the female spiritual journey is to take back what she has given away: her voice, her intuition, and *her fullest self*.

She must come face-to-face not with her limits, *but instead* with the enormity of her potential that has been pushed underground and put to sleep. She must confess the god-like status she has given to patriarchy, and repent, which simply means to turn. She must head in a new direction—one that faces a God who is truly for her, reflects her full self, and invites her into the journey of becoming most fully who she was created to be. Now, she can begin the journey of ascent, courageously taking up all the space that was designated hers from eternity.

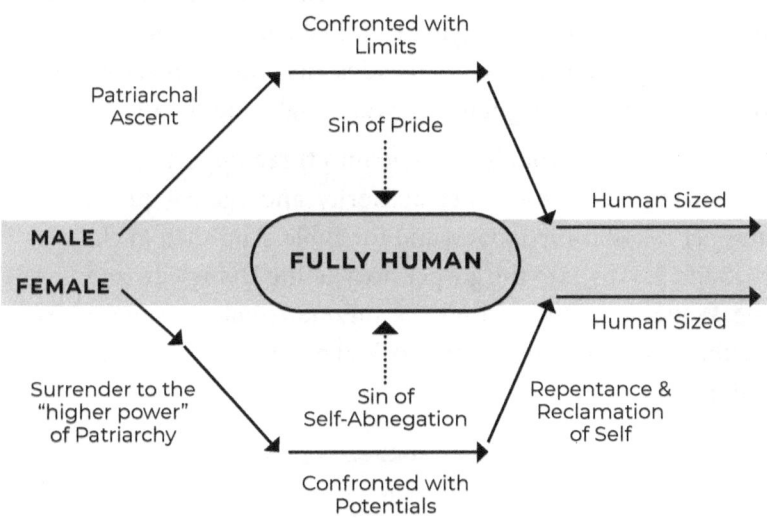

Make no mistake, this is hard and painful work. A liberating but lengthy journey. "What a long time it can take to become the person one has always been! How often in the process we mask ourselves in faces that are not our own . . . It is a strange gift, this birthright gift of self. Accepting it turns out to be even more demanding than attempting to become someone else!"[19] To truly face our potential, and confidently own and steward our greatness will be, in some senses, harder and more disruptive than simply accepting the limitations of patriarchy. We will be rejected, written off and labeled as a threat. We will be seen as selfish, or even worse—given the scarlet letter of Christianity and branded a heretic.

We will endure seasons where, like the Israelites leaving Egypt, we will want to cry out, "It would have been better to stay and serve the [patriarchy] than to die in the desert" (Exod. 14:12). But if we remain—*if we stay awake*—the very place that seems certain to bring about our imminent death will instead offer us the deepest of invitations. The desert wilderness is exactly where we must go to meet the hidden and unclaimed parts of ourselves. As soon as we can look beyond the surface and dig down, we will be met with the force of a whole life waiting to be unleashed, and an inner compass that already knows the way. Consider this book your shovel. If you move forward and begin to dig, what might you discover?

In chapters 2 through 4, I dive into three important aspects of a woman's reclamation: her authority and agency, her full self, and her relationship to God and the Bible. And then in chapters 5 through 8, I dig into the gospel story of the Dying Girl and Bleeding Woman, where we find the unique female spiritual journey outlined by Jesus' invitations to Wake Up, Stand Up, and Come Out of Hiding.

As it turns out, my childhood balloon flying up to the heavens had more significance than I knew. It has been a necessary journey to find God in all places so that I, a woman, might eventually see myself in the balloon, and release into a trajectory of moving up, up and awake. There is only one direction we're meant to head: into our full humanity.

So, who are you becoming on the journey of becoming you?

FOR FURTHER REFLECTION:

1. After finishing the chapter, take a few moments to be still and pay attention to what is stirring in you. What do you feel in your body? What emotions arise? Do you feel resistance of any kind? You don't need to solve anything. The invitation is to simply practice awareness and begin listening to your own embodied knowing.

2. When you consider your journey of becoming, in what ways have you been influenced by the buffet line mentality? Can you identify what is currently on your plate that doesn't belong there?

3. How would your relationship with yourself and with God look and feel different if you truly understood yourself to be God's Beloved, instead of inherently bad?

4. Which of the unhelpful road maps resonates most for you? How have these frameworks impacted you personally?

5. In what ways are you currently self-abnegating (acting in ways that reject and/or renounce the self)? Have a conversation about this with God, remembering that God is so very tender and kind toward you.

CHAPTER TWO

FULLY HUMAN

RECLAIMING YOUR GOD-GIVEN AUTHORITY AND AGENCY

Though her soul requires seeing, the culture around her requires sightlessness. Though her soul wishes to speak its truth, she is pressured to be silent.

— Clarissa Pinkola Estés[20]

We are easy to shame, eager to prove our worthiness, to seek validation from some power outside of ourselves.

— Elise Loehnen[21]

When I was eleven, a man at church came up to me and told me that I needed to dress differently. I was causing him to stumble.

— Former coaching client

ONE of my all-time favorite TV shows is *This Is Us*, a drama series that tells the emotional story of the Pierson family. The writers beautifully display how the story of any one person is the unfolding of a generational story—that who we are, and who we are becoming, cannot be isolated in time. We are all inextricably linked, particularly within families. It's why websites and resources that link us to our ancestry have become so popular. We instinctively know that our stories exist on a continuum, and our stories matter because they tell us who we are and what might become of us.

Who am I? Who am I becoming? No human can escape these two questions, and every human—whether aware of it or not—has an answer. We each have an identity and a trajectory, both continuously formed by the various realities and choices of our lives. The fancy term for this process is spiritual formation.

As Dallas Willard wrote, spiritual formation "is a process that happens to everyone. The most despicable as well as the most admirable of persons have had a spiritual formation. Terrorists as well as saints are the outcome of spiritual formation."[22] This process of spiritual formation, or what I like to refer to as the "journey of becoming," is not reserved for those who identify as religious, or who have chosen a particular life path. *Everyone* is being spiritually formed. Much of this process is unconscious, happening outside of our awareness by millions of intersecting factors making up our unique individual lives and beliefs. Factors like our place in history, where we live, the people in our circles, what we are taught in school and by our religion, the unique experiences we each have, our interests, and the habits we keep—all of these (and much more) play a part in forming who we are becoming.

Much can be learned from a person's reflections at the end of life, but what a tragedy if one's deathbed is the first time one honestly looks at and examines their path. Life's invitation to pay attention, looking lovingly and truthfully at the realities of our lives, comes long before the end. All that is shaping our identity and trajectory need not remain unconscious. An intentional journey of becoming is possible as we choose to pay attention; an intentional *Christian* journey of becoming is possible as we pay attention through a Christ lens.

Christian spiritual formation is often associated with 2 Corinthians 3:17-18 which says, "Now the Lord is the Spirit, and where the Spirit of the Lord is, there is freedom. And we all, who with unveiled faces contemplate the Lord's glory, are being transformed into his image with ever-increasing glory, which comes from the Lord, who is the Spirit." The classic definition can be summed up from these verses in the following way: *Christian spiritual formation is the process of being conformed to the image of Jesus Christ for the glory of God and the sake of others.*[23]

This definition points toward a process of paying attention to our lives and engaging what we see in a way that frees us to become more and more like Jesus. It's a mysterious and beautiful becoming, that happens as we partner with the Holy Spirit's work in our lives. It is both internal and external, abounding with grace. And its purpose is our good, for the good of the world.

In my time studying, but more so as I have functioned over the years as a practitioner of spiritual formation, I have found that tweaking the classic definition has been important, especially as it pertains to the female spiritual journey. The definition I offer is this: *Christian Spiritual formation is the process or journey of becoming most fully human, most fully who God created us to be. Jesus is our model and lens.*

Although there is nothing inherently wrong with the classic definition of Christian spiritual formation, I'm afraid that some of our bad theological habits have led us astray. We've been taught to believe our trajectory ought to move us away from our humanity (which is seen as flawed), move us out of our bodies (which are assumed untrustworthy), and make us afraid of focusing on our unique design (which gets a little too close to navel gazing).

This chapter is all about the reclamation of our full humanity as women—an impossible endeavor if we have bought into a spirituality that assumes being human is inherently bad, disembodied, and one-size-fits-all. The female spiritual journey requires a robust spiritual formation that understands being fully human as the goal, not the problem, and can acknowledge that to be human is both embodied and unique.

The Goal, Not The Problem

In the book of Genesis, Creator God brings a whole plethora of life forms into existence. Among the teeming organisms and creatures, only one is given the privilege of being like God. Genesis 1:27-28 reads, "God created humans in God's image, male and female God created them." It's truly something to say that in our humanity—in our very flesh and blood—*we are like God.*

Perhaps it's even more astounding to consider that the God whose image we are made in became like *us* in the person of Jesus. In *The Divine Conspiracy*, Dallas Willard explains the significance of this reality:

> . . . He was an ordinary workman: a "blue-collar" worker. He did all this to be with us, to be one of us, to "arrange for the delivery" of his life to us . . . If he were to come to us today as he did then, he could carry out his mission through most any decent and useful occupation . . . In other words, if he were to come today he could very well do what you do. He could very well live in your apartment or house, hold down your job, have your education and life prospects, and live within your family, surroundings and time. None of this would be the least hindrance to the eternal kind of life that was his by nature and becomes available to us through him. *Our human life, it turns out, is not destroyed by God's life but is fulfilled in it and in it alone* (italics mine).[24]

The very fulfillment of our life in God happens not despite our humanity, but with our humanity as the very container. So, why does being human get such a bad rap?

In Chapter One, I discussed how original sin—the belief that humans are inherently sinful—creates a scarcity narrative, resulting in a hierarchy that ultimately leaves women at the bottom and competing for place. But there is another way in which our understanding of what it means to be human, and a woman, gets twisted.

Dehumanization is the process in which a person or a group is perceived and treated as less than fully human. Broadly speaking, it involves the denial of human attributes or characteristics. This denial takes one of two forms. *Animalistic dehumanization* is when a person is denied uniquely human attributes like civility and rationality, and therefore likened to an animal. *Mechanistic dehumanization* is when a person is denied human attributes such as warmth, emotionality, and vitality, and therefore likened to a machine.[25] Once the person or group is seen as something other than human, it somehow makes "logical" allowances for unjust treatment. Sadly, Christian history has its fair share of practicing this.[26]

In Chapter One, I presented statements from some of the early Church's Fathers about women. Take a closer look at a couple of those examples, shown below, and notice how dehumanization is reflected in the phrasing.

- Animalistic Dehumanization: "St. John Chrysotom's word: 'Among all **savage beasts** none is found so harmful as woman'" (emphasis mine).[27]

- Mechanistic Dehumanization: "Thomas Aquinas referred to woman as '**misbegotten male**' and held that women would not have been created at all had they not been **required for the service of men**" (emphasis mine).[28]

Chalking these beliefs about women up as merely an extreme complementarian viewpoint is a gross disservice (and ought to offend anyone who identifies as a complementarian).[29] These men were active participants in the dehumanization of women, acting contrary to what the scripture itself has declared. To be human is to be made in the image of God: "male *and female* God created them" (Gen. 1:27-28).

The treatment of women as beloved image-bearers of God ought to be a high priority for the Christian Church. However, the stark reality for much of Christian history is that to be a woman has meant to be less than human. These are not simply parts of our past, but very real factors that have deeply formed the faith passed down to us. Whether we are conscious of it or not, these views still impact us, seared into our consciousness even in the most seemingly progressive of spaces. We may even say we affirm women in Christian leadership, but allow our preferences for a traditionally male way of structuring church and spiritual development to filter how we make decisions. The whole premise of this book is that we have unquestionably accepted patriarchy as a God-breathed framework for our lives, ultimately discounting the made-in-the-image-of-God, full humanity of women.

In my season of serving in leadership at the post-evangelical church—not long after we had walked through the process of LGBTQIA+ inclusion—our leadership was invited to visit a local place of worship. The evening before the visit, an email was sent out giving directions and expectations for the time. There was one particular detail we needed to be prepared for. At some point, the women would stay in a specific area while the men moved on. Women did not have permission to fully participate. Was I surprised by this? No. Had this happened two years or ten years prior, I would have thought nothing of it. But this was different. *I was different.* I found myself shocked, not by what was expected of women, but by the response of "my tribe."

No one flinched. No eyes batted. No pushback. And the lack of reaction hit me like a ton of bricks. Here was a group of people I had just spent an extended season with, pouring ourselves out to one another and smashing old paradigms to create a wider and more welcoming table. I knew deep in my bones that if that email had communicated something a little different—that some other group or classification of people would not have permission to fully participate—every single person in that group would have stood up and said, "Wait a second. We can't and won't accommodate that ask." *And rightly so.* But for some reason, when it came to women, we were . . . *used to it?* We expected it? Or maybe it had just become so ingrained in us, we couldn't see it as a problem. This was the day I woke up to just how subtle, hidden, and insidious patriarchy and the Church's dehumanization of women is.

We must be wise stewards of the faith tradition we have been handed, diligently paying attention through our Christ lens as we confess and root out that which is contrary to God's *actual* view of humanity. Healthy spiritual development will go out of its way to affirm women's full humanity, confirm that they are inherently good, and invite them to step most fully into who God created them to be.

Embodied

In the gospel of John, chapters 14-17, we find what is known as the farewell discourse. Jesus says his goodbyes as he moves toward his imminent death, and prepares his disciples for what's to come. Jesus said to them:

> And I will ask the Father, and he will give you another advocate to help you and be with you forever—the Spirit of truth. The world cannot accept him, because it neither sees him nor knows him. But you know him, for he lives with you and will be in you . . . But very truly I tell you, it is for your good that I am going away. Unless I go away, the Advocate will not come to you; but if I go, I will send him to you. (John 14:16-17; 16:7)

Think for a moment about how disorienting this must have been for the disciples. How could there be a better scenario than Jesus' physical presence with them? And what did he mean by this business of sending another—one that the world could not see, and would not only be with them, but *in* them? What Jesus said to the disciples is both confusing and ultimately astounding.

The promised presence of God wouldn't have been a new idea for the disciples. They knew the story of those who had gone before them. In the Old Testament, the Israelites understood themselves to be the people of the Presence: the ones among whom God had chosen to dwell (Exod. 19). And, the most prominent way in the Old Testament that God's presence was experienced was through the Tabernacle and the Temple, structures where God's presence descended upon and filled like a cloud.

But when Jerusalem fell and the temple was destroyed, the Israelites were no longer a people distinguished by the presence of the living God, as described in 1st and 2nd Kings. They longed for the day, promised in the prophetic books such as Joel 2:28, when they would once again experience God's presence with them. The disciples had experienced Jesus' physical and very personal presence. They could touch and talk with Jesus. And he wasn't confined to a specific place or structure. Was this not the fulfillment of the promise? Why was Jesus leaving and how could any other form of God's presence with them be better than what they were given in the embodied Christ?

Thankfully, we have the gift of knowing the whole story, beyond the gospel of John. In Acts 2, on the day of Pentecost, a very bizarre situation happens. A sound like the blowing of a violent wind filled the room where the disciples had gathered. They saw what appeared to be tongues of fire that separated and rested on each of them, and suddenly all of them—*the people*—were filled with the Holy Spirit and began to speak in other languages (Acts 2:1-4). The Advocate had come, just as Jesus said.

Now again, consider this within the context of their history. Whereas the presence of God in the Old Testament had descended upon and filled the tabernacle and temple, here the presence of God descended upon and filled the disciples. God's promise to dwell once again in and among his people was fulfilled, and plot twist—*the dwelling place of God now was God's people.*

What could be more accessible and intimate than having Jesus' physical presence with you? How about the God of the universe making their dwelling place *in you*? Paul continues to affirm this reality, calling our body "the temple of the Holy Spirit" (1 Cor. 6:19) and proclaiming that the Spirit who raised Jesus from the dead lives in all of us (Rom. 8:11).

That is some substantial power. In you. *In your body.*

God doesn't exist in us in some ethereal, out-of-body experience kind of way. Our being the dwelling place of God is much grittier than that. More grounded and tactile. More *embodied.* To be human, made in the image of God, on this side of Pentecost, is to—in our very flesh and blood—hold an astounding amount of authority.

So, what happens to a woman when her whole life she is subtly (and sometimes overtly) given the following messages: your body cannot be trusted, and authority exists outside of you?[30] How does this form her and impact her answers to the questions, "Who am I?" and "Who am I becoming?" When a woman is taught that this is the truth of her existence, she is set on a trajectory other than made-in-the-image-of-God, temple of the Holy Spirit, human. I don't mean to imply that she somehow actually becomes "un-human." However, when we believe a lie about our humanity and about the way God/the world works, the natural outcome is to behave in inhumane ways. This is now my working definition of sin: whenever we act in ways that resist who God created us to be. I would argue that for men, who tend to hold more power, their inhumane behavior is more likely to move outward toward others and manifest in seeking dominance. For women, who are told they must be less than they are, their inhumane behavior is more likely to reach inward and manifest in denying the self.

When a woman is taught to believe that her body is inherently untrustworthy and that authority only exists outside of her, she is seemingly cut off from her Source (the Holy Spirit who dwells in her). She does not learn to listen to and act on her God-given authority and agency. Her inner-knowing may whisper in her ear, surface in her dreams, pound in her heart, or flutter in her gut, but too often her environment squashes any possibility of expressing this wisdom in her life . . . if she hasn't already squashed it herself first. She learns to live as if authority only exists outside of her. She must defer to other sources: church, institutions, leaders, men, or even other women. Ultimately, she does not believe authority is innately in her.

One way to counter this is by introducing women to contemplative practices, like the Prayer of Examen, which invite us inward, and assume our God-given ability to hear from the Divine, *through our body*.[31] We need to be taught how to discern the movement of God within ourselves as we use our senses, paying attention to our emotions, and trusting that we have wisdom to collect in these places. Unfortunately, many of us have been handed a spirituality that exists primarily between our heads and the clouds, overly cognitive and transcendent at the expense of being fully embodied and imminent. Women need to be invited back to themselves, back to their bodies, and back to their God-given authority. In embodied spirituality, we come out of our minds and back into our bodies, trusting that authority dwells there.

Unique

For over a decade, I have guided clients through a vocational discernment process. For two, eight-hour days, I guide women to listen to their lives—their stories, their preferences, their unique design—to help them name and take ownership of who God has created them to be. When you spend this many hours with this many women in this kind of context, you begin to see some common themes.

Generally speaking, for women who have grown up in or now find themselves in Christian culture, the theme of self-abnegation is overwhelmingly present. Patterns of playing small, holding back, waiting for permission, being overly apologetic, choosing pleasantries over truth-telling, avoiding and suppressing emotions like anger, feelings of invisibility, and imposter syndrome abound. Maybe you can relate.

In particular, a huge obstacle for many Christian women to overcome is our (mis)understanding of "roles" and how narrowly these have been defined. In answering the questions, "Who am I?" and "Who am I becoming?" women have been given very limited options, and it is clear that some options are more highly regarded than others.

Traditionally, if a woman can earn the roles of wife and mom then she is deemed good and fruitful, and is generally more culturally acceptable, particularly in churches. But is the sum of a woman truly found in whether she is married or not? If she is a mother or not? Is this not another form of mechanistic dehumanization, making a woman's primary indicator of identity her usefulness in these specific roles?

I'm a wife and mom—proudly, gratefully, humbly. However, I'm not looking to center a conversation about marriage and motherhood that too often becomes a distraction from what's *actually* at the heart of every human's purpose: their unique design. And so instead, I want to focus on how "roles" became primary in the conversation about a woman's purpose, where it should be secondary.

I'm going to introduce a term to our conversation that may trigger some cringe, some confusion, or some mix of the two: *Calling.* Before I define this term, let's name what it isn't. Calling is not something that happens when you feel it's time to end a relationship ("God is calling me to break up with you"). It is not the urge to go on a mission trip ("God is calling me to another country"). It's not reserved for people in full-time ministry ("God is calling me to become a pastor"). It's not even the specific job or role you may feel destined for ("I'm called to be a mom, doctor, teacher, etc."). I'm going to take a gamble and assume that the last line is bringing up some resistance in you, and for good reason.

The word calling comes from the Latin word *vocatio*, meaning "a call or summons." There is another word we use that derives from *vocatio*: vocation.[32] Technically, the terms "calling" and "vocation" can be used interchangeably, however, let me ask you something. What comes to mind when you hear the word vocation? What do you assume this word represents? I'm counting on your answer being something along the lines of a job. In modern parlance, we commonly use the word vocation to mean work.

It was Martin Luther, in the Protestant Reformation, who first taught that one's vocation was equal to their job or occupation.[33] He was reacting to, and attempting to correct, the idea that calling was only reserved for "priests, nuns, and monks," a distortion birthed out of the Catholic Church of the time.[34] He wanted to emphasize that all work—even work outside the Church—was considered holy, and that all people—even those who were not clergy—had a calling. However, the impact of this "correction" turned out to narrow rather than widen the field. Theoretically, calling was once again accessible to all people, but the meaning of "calling" had narrowed significantly. Os Guinness refers to this shift as the "Protestant Distortion," which just replaced one form of dualism with another. Rather than the sacred being elevated at the expense of the secular, now the secular became elevated at the expense of the sacred.[35]

What may have been a latent imbalance earlier grows

steadily in the Puritan era into a full-grown distortion. Slowly such words as *work, trade, employment,* and *occupation* came to be used interchangeably with *calling* and *vocation* . . . the original demand that each Christian should have a calling was boiled down to the demand that each citizen should have a job.[36]

Calling was always meant for everyone, but what was originally understood as one's purpose, defined by God and discerned by the intimate exchange between the Caller and the one called, now shifted to mean one's responsibilities as defined by a job or role—not who they were, the gifts they had, or the offerings they could bring to a space.

How did this impact women both then and now? In her book *The Making of Biblical Womanhood: How the Subjugation of Women Became Gospel Truth,* Beth Allison Barr explains how Reformation Theology served to "strengthen and reinforce" what came to be understood as "Biblical Womanhood," which Barr describes as, "the belief that God designed women to be submissive wives, virtuous mothers, and joyful homemakers."[37] This wasn't always the norm. In fact, Christian history includes a time when the exact opposite was true. Women were once taught that their "primary calling was to serve God first, which for some meant eschewing traditional family life and for others meant working around it."[38] Referencing Lyndal Roper's work, Barr explains that in Reformation Theology, "The language of God . . . married the gender hierarchy of early modern Europe, and subordinate wifedom became synonymous with being a godly woman."[39] This sealed the deal. If one's calling meant one's work, then a woman's calling or work was to be a wife and mother.

Certainly, the roles we find ourselves in and choose are important, and how we interact with them will be one of many factors forming our answers to the questions "Who am I?" and "Who am

I becoming?" But we must be careful not to live as if these roles are the answers. As Gordon T. Smith points out in his book *Courage and Calling: Embracing Your God-Given Potential*, "we must not allow a singular career or occupation to eclipse our identity and sense of vocation. The two must be kept distinct." [40]

It's quite logical, if you think about it. I mean, if someone retires, do we assume they no longer have a calling? In the world of multi-careering, would we say that someone has multiple callings? What about the person who finds themselves unemployed? *Better hurry up and get a job so your existence matters again!* What happens to a woman whose children graduate, get married, or move away? And then of course, what of the woman who is never married? What about the one who can't or chooses not to have children? Do their lives seriously lack calling? It all feels a bit silly to me. Roles may come and go, morph over time, or never be had at all, but who a woman is, and is becoming, stays intact.

So, if our occupation/roles are not our calling, then what exactly is? And why is the water so seemingly muddied on the topic?

At the heart of calling is an individual's unique design. Every human is created in God's image, reflecting who God is uniquely, and has been given the capacity to explore and know themselves and their own distinct God-reflection. David G. Benner describes this as our "one possible way of being that carries with it the gift of authenticity."[41] Ultimately, calling is not about a specific role, but rather a unique style of being in the world. It's the one-of-a-kind way we respond to the voice of the Caller with the dance of our lives.

One's unique design is made up of many facets, including (but not limited to) their core talents, heart passions, core values, preferences, temperament, and distinct story/life experiences. Those combined create our calling.

The idea of calling is central to the work I do with vocational coaching clients. In one of the exercises we create a life purpose statement that begins with, "I exist to . . . " At the outset, the exercise can feel overwhelming for a client. The idea of this statement feels so big. Too big. *How can I possibly nail down exactly what I am created for?* Much of the anxiety is attached to what we have been taught about calling. They assume this statement is going to name the exact job or role they are supposed to have. They might be tempted to write something like, "I exist to be a mother," "I exist to be an attorney," or some other specific job. *But that's not what calling is.* Instead, this statement is meant to get at our essence, broadly speaking to how it is we make our way through the world. It's meant to summarize how we uniquely show up, with our particular talents and heart passions—our God-given "what" and "why."

My personal life purpose statement goes something like this: *I exist to guide others to connect the parts to the whole in order to engage the formation and integration of their truest selves.* The language I use here isn't random. It's not pulled out of the air just because I like the way it sounds. This statement represents layers and layers of who I am, my unique story and experiences, and what I care most deeply about. I first began to craft this statement over a decade ago. Along the way, I have added and tweaked as I have listened to my life and gained more clarity on my God-given design. This statement doesn't tell me exactly what job or role to have, *but it does inform it.* In fact, it informs any and all roles I have. I am at my best as a mom, wife, friend, neighbor, worker, and citizen when I am filtering my yeses and nos in all these areas of life through this statement.

One's calling reflects a God who takes us seriously and who expects us to do the same. Good stewardship of our lives will require knowing ourselves and utilizing this self-knowledge as we discern both what roles we pursue, and how we show up to the roles we inherently have. A life of faithfulness is one of congruence where our yeses and nos increasingly match our God-given unique design.

I would argue that much of our confusion around calling stems from a resistance to lovingly look at the self and understand the deep, complex facets that inform our unique design—our essential being that differentiates us from others. We don't know ourselves. We may not have a clue of how to finish the sentence: "I exist to . . ." And so, we let roles define our calling, and stop there. For women, this resistance is layered. Christian culture has often designated the work of self-awareness as navel-gazing—a selfish endeavor. Anything labeled as "self-help" is considered suspect, and often approached with mistrust. Focusing too much on ourselves is self-centered. And this only becomes more complicated with an unhealthy emphasis on needing to be a wife and mom. To spend time on oneself not only makes you selfish, it also means you must be neglecting your other responsibilities. And no one, especially in Christian circles, wants to be labeled a bad mother or wife.

Much "course correction" is needed for both men and women in this area. However, it cannot be overstated just how uphill the battle is for women specifically. I agree with Carol Lakey Hess that in Christian spaces, "the promotion of self-sacrifice occurs for women before there is a self to give away."[42] The messaging for girls to self-abnegate begins early—long before she is capable of forming a sense of self. And so, for a woman, the journey of learning to look lovingly at the self to discern her unique design must begin with acknowledging the ways in which she has surrendered to a system that only deems parts of herself as acceptable, and then continue into rediscovering those discarded parts.

If we first filter our questions of "Who am I?" and "Who am I becoming?" through the seemingly available/acceptable roles before considering our unique design, we then have to decide what to do with the parts of us that don't fit in those prescribed roles. *I have leadership gifts, but I don't see women leading. I love being outside and playing in the dirt, but girls aren't supposed to get messy. I feel strongly, but when I express myself I'm told to be more polite. I'm a mom, but I really love my job.* As a result, we hide, get small, and ultimately put those seemingly incongruous pieces of ourselves to sleep. Over time, we may lose memory of these parts altogether, or assume they were just part of some childish dream, a "pre-role" us. To reclaim our full self will be some of the hardest work of the female journey—a full-on search and rescue operation of our unique design before the role told us who we were.

Every September, I help co-facilitate a soul care retreat in Spain called "Fully Awake: An Immersive Learning Experience for Women." The time is designed to help participants interact with the invitation to live fully awake to God and themselves, resisting the temptation to fall back asleep. A charming little town along the Mediterranean Sea acts as the backdrop for a time of exploring the often unexplored parts of self. As magical as jumping in the sea and eating incredible food around a gorgeous table can be, we have found that some of the most important learning and transformation comes not in Spain, but long before a woman ever even shows up to the retreat. The real seeds of transformation are planted in the process of simply saying yes to participating. It's astounding to consider the amount of roadblocks a woman must work through to convince herself it is okay, appropriate, and even good to say yes to her own self and soul care. It seems as if she might just let her whole village down with one decision to travel for a week, abandoning the roles she's promised to fulfill.

To break these old and unhelpful patterns, women need to be invited into and affirmed (over and over and over) for taking the life-long journey of reclaiming, knowing, and faithfully stewarding the self, in all her God-given unique glory.

Jesus: Our Model and Lens

If spiritual formation is the process or journey of becoming most fully human—most fully who God created us to be—what then will serve as our compass, directing us along the path and showing us the way? In Christian spiritual formation, it is Jesus in the Gospels who offers us a model, and Christ in us who becomes our lens.

Too often, we get so caught up in looking for principles, rules, and doctrine to pull and reflect on from Jesus' life that we forget how he also shows us what it is to be fully human. My friend Cari likes to read through the Gospels looking for Jesus' embodied humanity. She'll ask questions like, "What and how does Jesus *see*?" and then sets out to find and learn from each instance, learning from Jesus' moments as a human. I encourage you to try it for yourself. Spend some time reading through the gospels and ask questions like these:

- How does Jesus use his senses? What does he see, touch, hear?
- What emotions does he feel and express?
- How do we see Jesus attaching and attuning to others?
- How does he interact with people and what kinds of questions does he ask?
- What was Jesus' calling and how does he faithfully pursue it?
- How do Jesus' yeses and nos align with what he knew he was made for?
- How does Jesus listen to, and act on, his own embodied knowing?
- In what ways did Jesus care for himself?

Reading the gospels in this way offers us a masterclass in being fully human, but it's not our only guide. As Christ-followers, we have been given an additional source of insight: *Christ in us.* What a peculiar, mind-boggling truth. I'm not sure any of us fully understand what this means, but we know that Jesus promised us an Advocate (the Holy Spirit) and that the epistles speak of Christ living in us (i.e. 2 Cor. 13:5). It's as if we each have been given an internal homing device—what Paul seems to refer to as "the eyes of the heart" (Eph. 1:18). We have access to an inner knowing through our Christ lens.

In a world where women's bodies are assumed untrustworthy and void of authority, women have typically been given a patriarchal lens to put on. We've been handed a pair of glasses and told that our ability "to see" is dependent on wearing them. They filter how we view ourselves, the world, God, and the Bible. We are led to believe that if we take them off, we will lose our way. In a patriarchal world, these glasses are convincing because they help us to navigate a particular patriarchal way. They show us how to stay safe, acceptable, and relatively conflict-free within the system.

But what if the lens we need is already in us? And what if this points to our authority and agency? What if like Jesus—who modeled to us how to be fully human—we can commune with and hear from God directly? Women need to be encouraged to take off the patriarchal glasses, and given space to fumble around a bit on our own, even if we are initially disoriented by the lack of patriarchal guidance. If we can hang in there, we eventually come to see that we are fully capable of finding our way, and are even—dare I say—good at it. *We were* made for it, after all.

When the religious world is telling you there is a very specific patriarchal lens they would like you to put on and live by, no matter how good those glasses look or how much they help you to fit in, very kindly say, "No thanks. I can already see." And then go, and learn to trust your God-given authority and agency. Which is to say, learn to trust who God has created you to be.

FOR FURTHER REFLECTION:

1. After finishing the chapter, take a few moments to be still and pay attention to what is stirring in you. What do you feel in your body? What emotions arise? Do you feel resistance of any kind? You don't need to solve anything. The invitation is to simply practice awareness and to begin listening to your own embodied knowing.

2. Simple Examen is a simplified version of the Prayer of Examen and is a great practice for learning to trust our God-given authority and agency. It's meant to be a daily practice where you ask yourself two simple questions: When today did I feel most alive? When today did I feel most depleted? Another option of questions might be: When today did I feel most grateful? When today did I feel least grateful? Spend time every day for the next week (or even better, the next month) and journal through your answers. Pay attention to any patterns that emerge. Typically, what we feel most grateful for, or what makes us feel most alive is pointing toward what we need to cultivate more of in our lives (our yeses). Typically, what we feel least grateful for, or what tends to deplete us, is pointing toward areas we need to set limits on (our nos).

3. Set aside time to "lovingly look at the self." What can you name about who you are? What do you enjoy? What gives you life? What do you care deeply about? What parts of your God-given unique design can you identify? Be sure to take into account what has emerged in the practice of simple examen. Are there particular words, ideas, or themes that stand out and seem to speak to something important for you?

4. Consider how your understanding of "roles" has impacted your life trajectory. In what ways have you placed roles before calling, and what steps do you need to take to better discern what roles to say yes and no to, based on your unique design?

CHAPTER THREE

ALL OF YOU

RECLAIMING YOUR LOST AND HIDDEN PARTS

*Many of us have lived desert lives: very small on the surface,
and enormous under the ground.*

— Clarissa Pinkola Estés[43]

*As women we take a psycho-spiritual journey to become whole,
integrating all parts of our nature.*

— Maureen Murdock[44]

In my early thirties, I read a book where a daughter was recounting the experience of sitting at her mother's 60th birthday table. She described the women around the table, friends for years who could now, at 60, speak to and name the greatness of the woman celebrated. It was inspiring, and I immediately set out to piece together my 60th birthday table. Who will be *my* people?

Over the years, this image became a bit of a North Star for me. It informed my yearly goals. It filtered my yeses and nos. And for a while, this felt good and right. That is, until one day when I was confronted with the question: *Who gives a shit who is at my 60th birthday table, if I'm not fully there?*

This question didn't come out of nowhere. My reclamation—reclaiming my denied, rejected, and hidden self—had begun at this point. For a season, I had been deep-diving into naming and owning various parts of my identity, asking myself, "Who am I really, truly, fully?" For the first time, I was focused on not just my impact on others or the community, but how I felt about myself.

One day, some unexpected news surprised me with its force. An important person in my world was moving away. The news was sad, and it seemed to poke at something deep within that I hadn't yet known existed. As I paid attention to what it stirred in me, I began to reflect on my past and how this kind of event was a familiar part of my childhood—the feeling of being moved away from. Something was beginning to reveal itself. Some part of me, not-yet-claimed, was emerging. I invited others to accompany me in this: a few friends, a spiritual director for a time, and my therapist.

The first part of me that began to emerge as I explored these emotions was a wounded little girl: my Wounded Child. She is the most tender and vulnerable part of me. She longs to be seen, moved *toward*, and fought for. Somewhere along the way, I metaphorically set her on the shelf—out of harm's way—to protect her. It was my way of keeping feelings of vulnerability at bay, and keeping her big emotions under control when she felt someone moving away from her. But after years of being ignored, she was demanding to be heard.

To be exact, it was my False Self, the part of me created in response to early feelings of shame, who set her on the shelf. The "Holder-Together" is what I have come to call this part of me. She is steady, strong, and balanced. She has an uncanny ability to read a room and intuit the many dynamics, always noticing possible chaos and moving toward stability. She uses these superpowers to detect possible circumstances that might further bring out my Wounded Child.

For the season following the news that someone in my life was moving away, digging into and understanding the relationship between my "Wounded Child" and the "Holder-Together" was rich with discovery and insight. It was constant fodder for prayer and therapy sessions as I practiced living in a way that invited my Wounded Child down off the shelf where she could explore greater vulnerability and intimacy in relationships. I allowed my False Self to be held, rather than always doing the holding. This was good and necessary work, but it wasn't complete.

It would take a few more years, and just enough angst, to fully wake up to my female spiritual journey where I would uncover more parts of me to discover and name. These particular parts stayed hidden as long as I allowed my story to remain centered in a "man's world," wearing that patriarchal lens, and ignoring the deep yearning to know who I was fully. As Sue Monk Kidd says of her journey, "Nearing forty, I needed to rethink my life as a 'man-made woman.' To take back my soul."[45]

We live in a world where male is the default, and the patriarchal lens is the standard, especially in the "religion" domain. Unconsciously, women have learned to function in this world hidden and asleep, and the world is all too okay with this. In fact, a "man's world" depends on our hiding and sleeping to function as-is. When a woman begins to wake up, it can feel terrifying for her, and even for those around her. Why? Because women who wake up are disruptive, and this is the last thing a woman is supposed to be.

The disorientation of waking up propels us into a time of wandering and exploration as we attempt to make sense of what we are seeing for the first time. My waking moments began to invite me into the wilderness: seasons in my life characterized by spiritual dryness, doubt, a sense of lacking control, an uncertain future, etc. The invitation of this angsty desert place is to dig down and discover the wild enormity of your life that has lived underground. This is where my Wild Child began to emerge. She is me, but uninhibited, totally free, and living without hesitation. I have a picture that hangs above my desk of me as a toddler. My bright red hair stands out against my pale naked skin. I have no clothes on and am seemingly unfazed by this. It's a glimpse of my Wild Child, and what sunk underground early on in my life.

Our Wild Child is the part of us that says, "I need no better reason than my well-being to move fully into the world." She is the one who can tenderly laugh at herself, and not as some sort of sarcastic deflection. She is playful and curious. She is a truth-teller, but it's not the kind of truth you get to by thinking. It is truth by way of deep, intuitive knowing, and it can only be accessed as you learn to trust yourself. It is in this part of ourselves that we locate our God-given agency and authority. Our Wild Child doesn't wait for permission. She seizes it.

As I uncovered these parts of me, a conversation began between my False Self, Wounded Child, and Wild Child—a conversation meant to integrate more fully the parts of me that had developed throughout my life. I have often imagined them all sitting together at a table. Inevitably one would seem to be sitting at the head, facilitating the conversation, and leading from her unique vantage point. My False Self attempted to keep us safe and protected, my Wounded Child brought a sense of tenderness, and my Wild Child asked us to try something new and not be so afraid. It became a helpful check-in for me to consider: Who is there? Is everyone present and fully showing up?

If our table conversation primarily exists between our Wounded Child and our False Self, our inner dialogue will always be informed by parts of ourselves that have been created in response to others. We all have a Wounded Child and False Self, and inherently, these parts have incredible gifts to offer. They are keenly aware of the world around them and constantly assess next steps accordingly. When working in a healthy partnership, these two parts can be a force for incredible good in the world, shaping our most significant contributions. But, without the help of our Wild Child, they will continue to need a "why" outside of themselves, because they were developed in response to external factors. They will always look to an "outsider" for permission.

Table Dynamics: Who Sits at the Head?

One morning, I woke up with an explosion of uneasy feelings. I sat down on the couch to journal and center myself. I considered my table. Who was there? And what exactly was going on? I'd been having some pretty BIG feelings recently, and the various parts of me were all interacting and coping in their own ways.

For years, my False Self had sat at the head of this table. She took charge, careful to keep things neat and tidy. Calm and peaceful. As uneventful as possible. She took cues from the outside world, discerning what seemed safe and appropriate. After all, she is an excellent Holder-Together. For most of my life, she did the job I needed her to do. But as long as my False Self was in charge, my Wild Child would not fully show up. And with the work I had started to do, my Wild Child was begging to be let free.

As I surveyed the table on this uneasy morning, I found my Wounded Child crouched in a ball and hiding under the chair. My False Self was scolding my Wild Child who seemed to sit at the table hungover. She had been doing a lot of Wild Work lately. Everyone seemed to be out of sorts and in need of some T.L.C. The work I had been doing to take off the patriarchal lens was throwing everything off. Something was missing—a new part of me—to help sort this all out.

In *Soulcraft: Crossing into the Mysteries of Nature and Psyche*, depth psychologist Bill Plotkin explains that in adulthood, we must "relinquish attachment to the adolescent identity" and intentionally develop an additional sub-personality, or what he refers to as The Nurturing Parent.[46] In other words, these parts of ourselves that were formed in us as children (our Wild Child, Wounded Child, and False Self) can no longer run the show. Our table needs an adult voice who can lovingly direct our various parts as we go about living our lives.

This idea was so helpful to me. I began practicing a kind of inner conversation, led by my newly-developed Nurturing Parent. Using my journal, I would gently and kindly tell my False Self that she no longer needed to take charge. I looked at my Wounded Child with love and delight and reassured her it was safe to emerge, and I expressed my heartfelt desire and need for my Wild Child to fully and freely show up.

This bore fruit but still felt limited. This Nurturing Parent voice was coming from within me, and yet still seemed distant and detached. It wasn't until I was deep into an exploration of the Divine Feminine (the feminine imagery of God in the Bible) that it occurred to me. *I have kept my Nurturing Parent gender-neutral.* Which made me curious: *Why have I not related to this part of me as female . . . as Mother?* Looking for insight, I began to devour any resources I could find on women's development.

In *The Heroine's Journey: Woman's Quest for Wholeness*, Maureen Murdock explains that an important part of the female path includes healing what she calls the "Mother-Daughter Split."[47] This idea refers to the split from one's feminine nature, rooted in an imbalance of values in our culture, which hinders connection to both our mothers and to God as Mother. These imbalanced values and the invalidation of femininity send a clear message: to be female is inherently "less than." Unfortunately, it's an imbalance the church has been complicit in:

Our churches have pushed the feminine face of God underground for centuries, destroying her image and usurping her power ... How can we feel connected to the feminine when the culture around us does everything in its power to make us forget? We bow before the gods of greed, domination, and ignorance and scoff at feminine images of nurturance, balance, and generosity. We rape, plunder, and destroy the earth and expect her to give to us endlessly. This mother/daughter wound runs deep; it will take much to heal it.[48]

Sue Monk Kidd refers to this same idea as the "female wound," and describes her own experience in this way:

... As a woman, I was severed from something deep inside myself, something purely and powerfully feminine. Steeped in a faith tradition that men had named, shaped, and directed, I had no alliance with what might be called Sacred Feminine. I had lost my connection to feminine soul. When I use the term feminine soul, I'm referring to a woman's inner repository of the Divine Feminine, her deep source, her natural instinct, guiding wisdom, and power. It is everything that keeps a woman powerful and grounded in herself, and yet connected to all that is. Connection with this inner reality is a woman's most priceless experience.[49]

As humans made in the image of God, we make sense of who we are, and who we're becoming, in accordance with the image of God we're given. An absence of the Divine Feminine means we learn to relate to God as Father, but not Mother. Alongside a culture that reinforces this imbalance of values, girls are invited to function as daughters but are not given vision of an authoritative, divine, and *feminine* parental figure whose fullness they reflect. There is no clear path to womanhood. Rather than growing into a confident woman who experiences finding herself in the fullness of God, "we become the image of woman that the cultural father idealizes."[50]

We get stuck in the role of daughter, deferring to the cultural father at the center. This is problematic when we consider our need to grow up and cultivate an adult presence at our table.

Central to the unique female journey, and the reclamation of self, is the choice to de-center this cultural father figure, and courageously pursue the healing of our Mother-Daughter split. Only then can we develop our own inner Authoritative Nurturing Mother—the one who sits at the head of the table.

The Nurturing Mother is every feminine picture of God in how she relates to our Wild Child, Wounded Child, and False Self. She is a midwife, gently coaching and assisting us as we bring forth new life (Isa. 66:9; Ps. 22:9-10). She is like *Shekinah*, fully present and leading us forth in our wilderness journey (Exod. 40).[51] She is like a mother bear with her cubs, fiercely protective (Hos. 13:8). She is like a nursing mother, intimately connected to her child's needs, and bringing nourishment. Her children are never forgotten. (Isa. 49:15). She is like a mother eagle hovering over her young and spreading her wings to catch and carry them (Deut. 32:11-12).

I have come to affectionately call this developing part of myself "Mother-Me." In my living and my praying, I daily allow her voice to become central. Her tone, her nuance, her confidence. She is my hand that rests on my chest when I feel anxiety well up. She is the reminder to take a deep breath. She is the one who chooses to look for and receive the loving face of Mother God. She is the wisdom-seeker, the gratitude-gatherer, the presence-offerer. Deeply grounded in the Ground of Being, she is me at my best reflecting the fullness of God. And she is the final and central person on my table's guest list. I've got around 15 years until my 60th. Fifteen years to practice bringing each part of me fully to the table, with Mother-Me at the head.

So, *who's in charge of your table?*

My Story Within God's Story

How do we begin to listen to our lives in such a way that we might identify our various sub-personalities and invite them all to the table? Perhaps our own origin stories could be illuminated as we look at them against the backdrop of *the* origin story. I'm referring to Genesis, and a narrative about humanity: how humans came to be, and how they went into hiding.

In the beginning, God mixed a bit of muddy earth and Divine Breath. The Creator formed the first human and called this work of art *very good*. Before any performative act. Before any declaration of sound doctrine or belief. Before anything that might prove their worthiness, God speaks over humanity, *"very good"* (Gen. 2:7; 1:31).

As the story continues to unfold, God cultivates flourishing by providing humanity with purpose (Gen. 2:15), parameters (Gen. 2:17), and partnership (Gen. 2:18). All is well as is evidenced by the man and woman being totally naked, and yet without shame (Gen. 2:25). To be naked is, of course, to be totally nude, but the Hebrew word here can also mean "having no possessions." They are just them, shame-free and with no need to add anything external. At the end of Genesis 2, Adam and Eve are free to be their truest and fullest selves.

But no good story is complete without conflict. It isn't long before the serpent slithers onto the scene. The craftiest of all the creatures engages them in a lie, essentially telling them that in their nakedness they were in fact, *not* very good. They weren't enough, God had not given them enough, and *they could do something about it*. The man and woman believe the lie, eat the fruit, and their eyes are opened. Suddenly they are aware of themselves in a new way—one that breeds shame. They respond by covering up and hiding (Gen. 3:1-7).

God comes looking for them and begins asking questions:

Where are you? Who told you that you were naked? What is this you have done? (Gen. 3:8-13) If you pause and think about it, God (being God) surely already knows the answers to these questions. So, why ask them? If we understand this story as a framework or a story that represents us all, then God's questions become more perennial and timeless.

- **"Who told you that you were naked?"** Who told you a lie about yourself? And, what lie did they tell you?

- **"What is this you have done?"** What have you done in response to the lie? What have you decided about your identity?

- **"Where are you?"** Where are you hiding? What are you using to cover up your "not enoughness"?

These are the very questions we must engage if we are to identify our Wounded Child and False Self, or what caused us to go into hiding.

Naming Our Parts: Wounded Child and False Self

The Self is who you are and who you are meant to become. It is the image or unique face of God that has been set aside from eternity for you.[52] From the beginning, you are good, loved, and enough. However, we each have wounding experiences in our lives that have told us a lie about who we are and how we don't measure up—how we are *not* good, loved, or enough. In response to these wounds, our Wounded Child sub-personality is formed. Wounds are as varied and unique as we each are. One person's wounds aren't more important or valid than another. We *all* have a Wounded Child in us.

The False Self, then, is the part who believes the lie of our wounds and, just like Adam and Eve, covers the Self up with another identity to seek validation. Driven by shame, the False Self is a persona that works hard to be perceived in a particular way—so much so that we come to mistake this perception for reality. In many ways, the False Self is an illusion, but we learn to live as if it is part of our essential being. "Few things are more difficult to discern and dismantle than our most cherished illusions. And none of our illusions are harder to identify than those that lie at the heart of our false self."[53]

Our False Self was created unconsciously and remains unconscious unless we do the work necessary to uncover our covering. To reclaim our full Self, we must sift through and name the lies we have believed, and the false identities we hide behind in response to our wounding and shame.

Tools for the Journey: Wounded Child and False Self

Exploring our wounding feels like it sounds: *painful*. Some of us have spent more time considering our wounds than others. If this is new for you, please understand that the most important "tool" you will need in this exploration is trusted guides: friends, partners, therapists, spiritual directors, etc. Some of our wounding experiences have involved trauma and will benefit from (and at times require) the help of trained guides. I realize this is no small thing. It is such brave work to look for and initiate these kinds of relationships and then show up and offer your story. Our Wounded Child is our "emotional, sensual, playful, and vulnerable part."[54] She is a little girl, heart on her sleeve, and carrying the most fragile of wounding messages. We must approach her like we would any small, vulnerable child: tenderly, safely, and with the greatest of care.

Although we have experienced wounds throughout our lives, the most important in this work will be the very earliest. According to Bill Plotkin, our Wounded Child, and subsequently our False Self, likely developed around age two or three.[55] This typically means that working through our wounds requires a revisiting of all things related to our family of origin: dynamics, important stories and events, messaging, etc.[56]

For many years, I could easily explain the concept of the False Self, but couldn't tell you anything about my own. One summer, I was in a book club where we read David G. Benner's book, *The Gift of Being Yourself*. Benner's work is some of the best I've come across in its ability to not just help you make sense of *the* False Self, but make sense of *your* False Self. It was out of this book that I created a set of personal reflection questions.[57] For three months I committed to reflecting on, and journaling through the following questions:

1. What has caused me fear and anxiety today?

2. Of what or of whom am I most afraid?

3. What do I hoard or cling to out of fear and scarcity?

4. In the last week, when have I been defensive and why?

5. What about others seems to bother me most this week?

6. In the last week, what has made me feel most vulnerable/has made me want to run for cover?

7. What is the image of myself to which I am most attached?

I asked God to help illuminate my False Self and I went to work. Each week, I gathered clues, and as inspired, would draw images in my journal. Increasingly, the image that stood out more than any other was that of my hands. I kept imagining them, clasped tightly together. Interestingly, it was during this time that I attended a contemplative prayer workshop where the facilitator invited us to examine our bodies. We were sitting in folding chairs, scanning from the top of our heads to the tip of our toes, simply noticing what we felt. I realized that almost every muscle in my body was contracted, even while sitting. I'm pretty sure if you had pulled out the folding chair from underneath me, I would have stayed in the exact spot and position. Here I was, being supported by a per-fectly good chair, and yet expending copious (albeit unconscious) energy to hold myself in place. From the imagery of tightly clasped hands to a prayerful body scan revealing my body's default posture, God was graciously showing me myself. I came to see that it was not just my hands I held tight, or my body, but my whole way of being. My False Self copes with wounding messages by working extra hard to hold everything together.

Although our False Self may appear to be strong or in control, we need to remember that she is very young. Once we can identify her and how she shows up, we must be careful not to reject or dismiss her. Instead, she needs to be reassured that the lies once believed are *lies* and that she is loved, good, and enough. And she needs to know that she still matters. The goal is not to get rid of her, but to reorient her—to offer her a new and more appropriate seat at the table.

Our Gift to Offer: Wounded Child and False Self

In vocational coaching, I walk clients through an exercise in naming their Turning Points. These are events that have shifted an internal or external reality. Once identified, I draw them out and the client is presented with a visual of their big life events. We then spend time observing and looking for clues about who they are from these Turning Points. Sometimes the client's wounding experiences show up. Sometimes they don't. Regardless, I have learned that one of the most important questions I can ask an individual is this: What did you need (in childhood) that you did not receive? More often than not, this question gets at early wounds, or our Wounded Child.

I needed to be seen.

I needed support.

I needed to be fought for.

I needed safety.

I needed to be enjoyed.

I needed to be believed in.

Our wounding is important in identifying our Wounded Child and False Self identities, but also because it will ultimately point us toward our greatest areas of passion, or what we care most deeply about. What we care about speaks to our unique design and calling. Typically, we most want to give the world that which we did not receive.

I want others to be seen.

I want to offer support.

I want to fight for others.

I want to be a safe person.

I want to enjoy others.

I want to believe in others.

Who is better to offer these particular gifts to others than ourselves? After all, this is the very pain we are most in tune with. Our life experiences have given us special antennae, making us hyper-aware of these specific needs as we pay attention to the world around us. When we begin to do the necessary work to bring health and healing to our stories, we are then able to freely offer our stories as a balm for the weary.

Additionally, our False Self reveals a treasure trove of our gifts and skills developed throughout our lives. What once was utilized to hustle for our worth can now simply be used to contribute to a good and meaningful life. Consider The Holder-Together, for example. In all my years of expending energy to hold everything together, many of my natural giftings have been illuminated, and I picked up several valuable skills: organization, strength, steadfastness, leadership, clear communication, preparedness, and learning. Exploring, identifying, healing, and reorienting our Wounded Child and False Self will ultimately help us to live more aligned, capable of offering who we uniquely are from a place of health.

Naming Our Parts: Wild Child

Our Wild Child is "our original sensual, magical, untamed self that has an essential relationship to the soul and is not interested in limiting itself in any way."[58] This is likely our most unexplored, and potentially intimidating part. As I see it, the Wild Child is interchangeable with the Self, and I believe that exploring the idea of our Self as our Wild Child is important, especially for Christian women. Nothing in our Christian experience has equated wild with good, at least not when it comes to being a woman. Wild is generally reserved for men, who are expected to be more rambunctious, encouraged to play in the dirt, and assumed to enjoy the outdoors. After all, "boys will be boys." To begin to traverse the wild terrain of our lives inevitably brings up fear and resistance for women, if not internally, then most certainly externally. There is a reason why Glennon Doyle's book titled *Untamed* was so popular, while also being blacklisted in most Evangelical spaces.

In my own experience, digging into and discovering my Wild Child has often been precipitated by wilderness seasons, and these seasons seemed to increase as I began moving toward and into mid-life. Beginning to integrate our Wild Child is developmentally appropriate in mid-life, as the task in this season of life for any individual—man or woman—is what Carl Jung called "individuation."[59] It is at this time of our lives that we must integrate who we are, distinguishing ourselves from others in healthy ways. But how can a woman begin to individuate if whole parts of herself remain hidden? Life has a way of bringing things to the surface through waking moments. The question is: are we ready? Will we expect it?

How will we respond? Will we push these moments back down?

Anxiety will inevitably accompany this part of the journey, as we come face-to-face with the enormity of our potentials long pushed underground. We must choose to befriend our anxiety, not be surprised when it shows up, and allow our uncomfortable feelings to wake us up to our actual lives. The alternative is to glimpse these pieces of ourselves, and fearfully fall back asleep.

Tools for the Journey: Wild Child

Exploring and identifying our Wild Child has many components. She contains all the parts and pieces of who we are that somewhere, in some way, were deemed unacceptable; areas we were told to "tone it down" or that were not considered appropriate. The unexplored terrain is vast. I am still early in this journey myself, and imagine there is much I have not yet discovered when it comes to Wild Work. From my vantage point, some important categories for women to consider are desire, creativity, sensuality/eroticism, power and authority, our relationship with our bodies, and our relationship with the outdoors (this list is by no means exhaustive). Whole books could be—and have been—written about each of these topics, and all are worthy of a woman's exploration as she embarks on her reclamation journey, but one, in particular, seems important in unlocking the rest.

Eroticism

Be honest. Some of you, as soon as you saw that there was a section titled "Eroticism," skipped right down to it. I don't blame you. This is the juicy stuff. The forbidden stuff. If you grew up in purity culture like I did, there is baggage to sort through and leave behind.[60] The body most certainly keeps the score, and I'm grateful to people who have done the hard work in naming what much of the outworking of purity culture was: trauma. However, I want to talk about more than just sex and the having, or not having, of it.

For me, "erotic" stirs up feelings of shame mingled with curiosity. It's a word I know better than to google images for. Many of us, when we signed on the True Love Waits dotted line, unknowingly signed away our ability to explore our own sensual selves and in doing so, buried much of our personal magic.[61] Psychotherapist, and respected expert on human relationships, Esther Perel, clarifies what eroticism is about:

> Eroticism is not sex per se, but the qualities of vitality, curiosity, and spontaneity that make us feel alive . . . The erotic landscape is vastly larger, richer, and more intricate than the physiology of sex or any repertoire of sexual techniques. It's the unexpected yet welcomed touch on a great first date; running into a dear old friend and absconding together for a drink; traveling to a brand new place and experiencing it unfold before you . . . Eroticism is cultivating pleasure for its own sake. It's about bringing adventure back into play and creativity into our lives.[62]

David G. Benner describes sexuality this way:

> Sexuality is the all-encompassing energy that is life itself. It reflects the fact that we are wired for love, intimacy and relationship. It is life surging within us and propelling us in the direction of not only love, friendship, family, and community but also generativity, delight, ecstasy, humor, union, and self-transcendence. It is an ever-present inner call to high-octane, passionate life—life that is lived not just in bed but also at work in all our relationships.[63]

Eroticism is so much more than a shameful act, it's a way of being— *of living fully awake.* In the name of decency and modesty, many of us have repressed whole parts of ourselves. Our Wild Child longs to come out and to cultivate a robust kind of life—one with vitality, curiosity, spontaneity, pleasure, adventure, play, creativity, generativity, delight, ecstasy, humor, union, self-transcendence—but she won't without our consent.

For our Wild Child to fully and freely emerge, we will need to redeem our understanding of and relationship to eroticism as defined above. We need to show our young untamed self that it is safe to come out—that we won't judge or reprimand her. A good starting place is to spend time exploring our early messaging. What were we taught about our body, pleasure, and sex? Were our desires considered trustworthy? If not, who or what was setting the parameters of our life—what we could and couldn't do? Give yourself permission to explore these topics (don't forget that permission is yours to give), and don't underestimate the power of simply asking yourself questions like: *What do I want? What do I enjoy? What brings me pleasure?* These don't have to be sexual in nature, but they can be.

Our Gift to Offer: Wild Child

It's simple, really. The gift of your Wild Child is . . . *you.* You, before your wounds and false beliefs started to take precedence. God created you, and before you could do or say anything, before you could impress, or hustle, or prove, God had already declared you to be "very good." The world is hungry for you to be you. When we give ourselves permission to be who we are—wild and magical— we inevitably invite the world around us to do the same. Isn't that what we all really want?

Developing and Inviting Our Nurturing Parent to the Table

The work of naming and reintegrating our Wild Child, Wounded Child, and False Self will not be possible without the cultivation of our Nurturing Parent. However, the beauty of developing your

Nurturing Parent is this: without realizing, you are likely already doing it. The fact that you picked up this book, and possibly worked through the previous sections, are all potential signs of your Nurturing Parent at work. She is actively gathering your parts, noticing who's missing, and who needs an invite to the table. Trust her. She has (your age here____) years of experience.

Help her as she creates personalized invitations for your Wounded Child, False Self, and Wild Child. In daily life, become aware of her, allowing hers to be the voice that speaks for you. Perhaps make it a regular practice to intentionally place her at the head of the table. Let her love and lead you. The younger parts of you long to hear her voice and receive her guidance.

When I guide women through the content found in these pages, I invite them to give names to and create actual images of each of their sub-personalities. I keep mine—four small, laminated cardstock circles—in the pocket of my journal. Sometimes, I will draw a table on a piece of paper and place each sub-personality where it seems to be located. In the middle of a stressful season, I will pull them out and check in with each—journaling through how they are each experiencing life, and what each needs to hear from my Nurturing Parent part. I encourage you to personalize this work as much as possible. The more clearly you can identify each sub-personality, the easier it will be to notice when and how they show up in your day-to-day life.

Your journey is not done. The work ahead will require much of you. At times it will feel terrifying in what it asks of you—the kinds of things that will put your False Self on full alert, expose the depths of vulnerability in your Wounded Child, and send your Wild Child back into hiding. Nothing will serve you more on this path than to cultivate your Nurturing Parent voice and establish her place at the head of your table. Trust me when I say this: you will not survive this journey without her.

The call to selfhood for a woman is incredibly important, but arduous work. Before we can begin the sacred task of reclaiming what we've given away, we must discover and name who we actually are.

It's no small thing to recover the lost and hidden parts of ourselves, fully welcoming them to the table. It is disruptive work that will challenge every assumption we hold, and expose every fear we painstakingly manage. Even so, it's worthy work, and it can't be avoided on the journey of becoming who God created us to be.

FOR FURTHER REFLECTION:

1. After finishing the chapter, take a few moments to be still and pay attention to what is stirring in you. What do you feel in your body? What emotions arise? Do you feel resistance of any kind? You don't need to solve anything. The invitation is to simply practice awareness, and to begin listening to your own embodied knowing.

2. Spend some time journaling through the False Self questions from David G. Benner. What kinds of clues do your answers offer you about your False Self?

    -   What has caused me fear and anxiety today?
    -   Of what or of whom am I most afraid?
    -   What do I hoard or cling to out of fear and scarcity?
    -   In the last week, when have I been defensive and why?
    -   What about others seems to bother me most this week?
    -   In the last week, what has made me feel most vulnerable/ has made me want to run for cover?

3. What is the image of yourself to which you are most attached?

4. What fears, if any, arise when you consider re-integrating your Wild Child? Where are you likely to experience resistance as you fully invite her "to the table"?

CHAPTER FOUR

MADE IN HER IMAGE

RECLAIMING GOD AND THE BIBLE

Taken together, psychologists' narrative research makes one resounding point: We don't just tell stories, stories tell us. They shape our thoughts and memories, and even change how we live our lives. Storytelling isn't just how we construct our identities, stories are our identities.

— Sadie F. Dingfelder[64]

As a child, my grandma would pay me to do Bible studies. While her tactics for evangelizing her grandkids didn't land well with everyone, they impacted me positively, and not just because I made enough money to buy dangly peace sign earrings. (Ironically, these were the same earrings she would buy from me later to keep me from wearing "broken crosses.") The truth is, I would have done the studies without being paid. I've always been drawn to the Bible, and genuinely interested in Jesus, never shying away from a good Bible study tool especially if it included underlining and highlighting.

I'll never forget in college when a campus minister saw me at a coffee shop studying my Bible and said, "good girl." *Literally,* this is what he said, and although it now gives me the creeps, at the time it affirmed a longing in me. I wanted to know and understand the Bible. I wanted to be the person I once heard about who had read the text so much he basically spoke in Bible verses all the time (the stuff of evangelical lore).

That was a lovely, innocent, *and kind of cringy* time.

If I'm honest, my relationship with the Bible has felt complicated for a while now. Maybe it's midlife. Maybe it's the post-COVID-19 world. Maybe it's carrying the grief of so much personal loss in this season. But even before that . . .

Maybe it was seminary, which sometimes gets called "cemetery" for a reason. Maybe it was asking big, hard questions about what I traditionally understood the Bible to say about the LGBTQIA+ community. Maybe it was the loss of friendship through political tumult (*are we even reading the same Bible?*). Maybe it was coming to understand biblical interpretation and how misogyny has been written into the text through gender exclusive language in versions like the ESV. Maybe it was law enforcement disrupting a peaceful protest in the wake of George Floyd's murder in order to clear a path for a photo op: Donald Trump holding a Bible in front of St. John's Church.

Let's just say that the lovely, innocent, and cringy relationship cultivated in my formative years has been replaced with something *much* more complicated. Somewhere along the way my relationship with the text became a lot less secure. What once felt concrete, unquestionable, and easily understandable has become something a bit more . . . *fluid.*

It's as if I learned to "swim," so to speak, in my early years, but at the time I perceived the container (the Bible) to be like a lap pool. There were clear markers for lanes, chlorine to kill anything seemingly harmful, and lifeguards waiting on the side. Without question, I trusted whoever had designed the pool and poured the concrete, most likely well trained and strong men. As long as I was in the pool, I would be safe. Eventually though, I realized—quite shockingly (and not without a good amount of disorientation)—that I was actually swimming in an ocean. It's not nearly as safe or contained as I once thought. It's much harder to explain the deep dark layers, the vast marine life, or the unfortunate amount of plastic that has made its way in. There seems to be more unknown than known. The question then becomes, is it worth it to stay in the water?

I believe it is.

To be clear, I don't mean for this to be a book about defending the Bible. Honestly, I gave up feeling like that was my job a long time ago. However, I know that for many women, the Bible has been used to demean, subjugate, and exclude our humanity. We've been given a story that is said to be sacred, but have not been fully invited in. We've been taught to interact with it in a very masculine, primarily intellectual way, while denying the possibility of a deeper embodied and more feminine knowing of the text. And, although women are made in the image of God, the primary God image we've been given does not actually look anything like us.

I find it unfortunate that the Bible has, in many ways, been co-opted. Just because a book has been translated and warped into a defense for patriarchy doesn't mean that that's what the Bible actually is. I guess we could just acquiesce, and I'm afraid that this is what more and more women are doing as they simply walk away. I don't blame anyone for feeling the need to do this, but I do want to advocate for something different, because I actually believe the Bible is a story for women too. What if part of the female spiritual journey is paying one last visit to the library that exists in your "man's world," stuffing the Bible in your backpack, and running like hell to get out of there? On second thought, just focus on running fast, and leave hell there in that library where it belongs.

If you struggle with the Bible, you are welcome here. It's an ancient book, with disturbing violence, that has too often been weaponized. I think these struggles, especially as women, are a good and natural part of our journey. We must ask honest questions, and fully feel the anger and confusion that comes with a big book full of masculine pronouns. After all, if the Bible is like an ocean, then just think how expansive God is. As much as some would like to make God out to be easily offendable, I'm quite confident that God is spacious enough to gently hold your angst.

If you don't struggle with the Bible, you are also welcome here. In my own journey, it wasn't until I made the choice to preach only in gender-inclusive terms (less about my own journey and more about the community I was helping lead) that parts of the Bible began to trouble me. Maybe this book will invite you into that place of unease. I'm sorry, and *welcome*.

Wherever you are, I ask that you might open yourself up to the Bible in fresh ways and to believe that it is possible to reclaim our relationship with Scripture, and with a God who is more like us than we've been taught.

Reclaiming Our Ability to Know God and The Bible

For centuries, women have brilliantly practiced the art of intellectual flexibility as we navigate primarily male language, imagery, structures, and the typical representatives of church and God. Commonly, female-specific topics or a focus on female Bible characters are reserved only for spaces like women's ministries, women's Bible studies, or women's retreats. I haven't heard many sermons that asked men to consider who they relate to more, *Mary or Martha*? And yet, as women, we are astoundingly good at finding ourselves in all kinds of male-centered stories and narratives—because they are the stories we hear about the most:

- I am the prodigal son, who returns home to the abundant love of the Father
- I am Peter, mustering up the faith to step out of the boat, and sinking as soon as I take my eyes off of Jesus

- I am John, the one whom Jesus loved

Intellectual flexibility is not a female specific skill. Women have just had more opportunities to develop it, particularly under patriarchy. I believe it's something men are also highly capable of, if given the chance and with the right amount of humility to lean in. Although intellectual flexibility is a valuable skill, women need to be invited into a different kind of relationship with the text. Not just as it pertains to male vs. female characters and pronouns, but the kind of relationship that utilizes our God-given authority and agency, and invites a more embodied and feminine knowing of the text.

How Do You Know What You Know?

What does it mean to know something? By what means do we come into understanding? In the modern Western world, we've been taught that the capacity to know something comes primarily through our ability to think. Our education system is built on this assumption, and the church functions much the same. We have often equated "faith" to checking off a list of beliefs, placing an extremely high value on doctrine and theology—what resides in our minds. Certainly, how and what we think matters, but is the emphasis on this one particular human capacity healthy?

Building on the work of Carl Jung, psychologist Eligio Stephen Gallegos identified what he called the Four Modes of Knowing: Thinking, Sensing, Feeling, and Imagery.[65] Each of these four modes are meant to be utilized, balanced, and integrated as one seeks to know. The four modes are equal in importance and power, and each is a distinct capacity that cannot be reduced to any of the others.

Sensing refers to everything we come to know through the use of our senses. I *know* that dinner is being prepared by the smell wafting down the hall. I *know* that it is still the middle of the night when I wake up and do not yet see the sun peeking through my window. I *know* that a pair of sweatpants are well-worn when I can feel the little fabric balls forming inside the pant leg. I *know* that another hour has passed when I hear the church bells ring. Of course, our sensing can become more sophisticated if we combine it with some level of emotional intelligence. When I see a particular look on someone's face I immediately *know* something is wrong. When I hear one's tone of voice, it offers me clues.

"Feeling is a mode of knowing energies, especially the energies governing our own physical and emotional movements."[66] It is the human capacity that energizes our action and reaction. It is through this mode that "an instantaneous knowing frequently happens, even though we may have no sensory evidence to substantiate such knowing."[67] Healthy and satisfying relationships are impossible without the human capacity to feel. We often struggle to trust our feelings because we've been taught that logic trumps all else. When we can't make logical sense of what stirs up inside us, we are likely to dismiss or downplay what this capacity is trying to tell us. According to Gallegos, "Thinking must learn that feeling has a longer and deeper memory than it does, and that it already *knows* why it is there. Thinking can learn to trust feeling and discover the 'why' later."[68]

Imagery is the mode that utilizes our imagination. It refers to our ability to form new concepts, images, and ideas that are not present to the capacity of sensing. This is the realm of dreams and visions, fairytales and parables. It's where symbols take on deeper meaning. Unfortunately in the Western world, "imagination has been contrasted with and pitted against truth and reality: '*It was just my imagination.*'"[69] It is interesting to note that although this mode may be discounted and seen as unreliable by some, the Bible is chock-full of imagery, metaphor, and symbol, and Jesus was a big fan of teaching in parables.

Thinking refers to our ability to know by means of logic, analysis and deductive reasoning. It is just as important as sensing, feeling and imagery, but becomes problematic when it functions as a primary mode of knowing, instead of equal with the other modes. According to Gallegos, we have been trained to view "thinking as the most valid way of knowing, in many cases *confusing* thinking with knowing, and accepting the other ways of knowing only in those interstices where they coincide with thinking."[70] But what if we saw and functioned in balanced ways that drew from all four of the modes? And how would this impact our relationship with the Bible and God?

For a season I served as a Spiritual Formation Pastor at a church that tended to attract those who were deconstructing their faith. Deconstruction most commonly refers to the process of taking apart what one has traditionally known faith to be, and particularly as it pertains to their "beliefs." Although some might quickly label this process dangerous, as a Spiritual Formation nerd, I understand it to be a very normal and developmentally appropriate part of the spiritual journey. Having said that, I do believe there's a way in which it can become dangerous.

If by deconstruct, we mean that we take apart a merely intellectual, thinking-mode understanding of faith, and then attempt to reconstruct by piecing together a new intellectual, thinking-mode understanding, this effort will fail . . . *every. time.* A thinking-mode understanding of faith is generally made up of precepts, propositional truths, and doctrine—something that could be presented as a list of beliefs to be checked off. To keep things purely intellectual is a mistake, and misses more holistic ways of knowing God and the Scripture.

Is it possible that more and more people are deconstructing only to never effectively reconstruct, because their faith was limited in terms of its knowing from the start? If the faith they have been handed is purely intellectual, and they've not been invited into knowing God through sensing, feeling, and imagery (or have been taught that these modes are inferior), then what is there to fall back on when some logical paradigm is called into question? What remains when a biblical framework they have relied on begins to show its gaps?

It's of interest to me that sensing, feeling, and imagery all require embodiment and a sense of inner authority. In a patriarchal-thinking world, the power to know is held externally and historically kept from women through lack of education or leadership opportunities. Patriarchy relies on sensing, feeling, and imagery being understood as inferior. Perhaps this is why an embodied way of knowing has traditionally been considered feminine, and treated as a liability or quickly dismissed. But what has been seen as a weakness in women (sensitivity and emotionality) is actually a superpower when it comes to comprehension. I would argue the current state of the church is broken in part because the very gifts needed to bring healing to the system exist in women who are diminished, made small, and counted out of influence.

When my thinking-based knowledge of God seems to fall apart under difficult questions or challenges (which in my experience has happened several times), I can lean on the deep embodied modes of knowing I possess. I have practiced a recognition of God in my sensing, I understand God to speak through my feelings, and because of rich encounters with imagery, I have come to understand God in ways that a propositional truth will never offer. All of this has required a deep trust in, cultivation, and awareness of my own God-given authority and agency—my own fully embodied knowing.

So how do we interact with Scripture and God in ways that invite all of our Modes of Knowing?

St. Ignatius and the Practice of Imaginative Prayer

I'm not sure any historical Christian figure (other than Jesus, of course) has had a greater impact on my own life and transformation than St. Ignatius of Loyola. Prior to being introduced to his work, I had a traditional, thinking-mode relationship with the Bible. I approached reading it like I would any other field of study: academically, linearly, logically. My goal was to know God, and this meant pulling out every truth I could find and then attempting to live a life that reflected those truths. I read, studied, and memorized, always ready to give an apologetic defense. Ignatius showed me another way, one where I could do more than just read about the story; I could imaginatively find myself *in* the story. Instead of studying the Scripture, I could invite the Scripture to study me.

In 1521, Iñigo López de Loyola, who would later take the name Ignatius, was severely wounded while serving as a commander in Pamplona, Spain. Struck by a cannonball, he found himself stuck in bed for several months post-surgery. In the 16th century, there was no "scrolling" or "streaming" to pass the time. Luckily for Ignatius, he had access to two books, and two books only: *Life of Christ* by Ludolph of Saxony and *The Golden Legend*, a collection of biographies on the Saints. Over and over, he read about the lives of Jesus and these Saints, but he didn't just read them, he fantasized about *being in* the stories themselves. In his imagination, Ignatius became people like St. Dominic and St. Francis of Assisi. He visualized living like they lived, and as he did something began to shift in Ignatius. His longings and desires transformed. Ignatius' conversion to Christ happened as he found himself in these stories, and then as his body healed, he enacted what first took place in his imagination. Immediately upon release, Ignatius began a pilgrimage to Jerusalem, giving away his nice clothes and taking on a robe of poverty as he started the journey.

Ignatius would go on to start a religious order, now known as the Jesuits. He wrote *The Spiritual Exercises of St. Ignatius*, a collection of prayers and meditations to become closer to God, which are still widely used today. Central to the *Spiritual Exercises* is the practice of Imaginative Prayer.

In the practice of Imaginative Prayer, the participant is invited to place themselves within the events of the life of Christ as though they are actually taking place and finding themselves there, like what Ignatius practiced when wounded and in bed for months. Imaginative Prayer invites a holistic engagement with the Scripture as it utilizes all four of the Modes of Knowing. The participant enters the exercise using **imagery**, and then pays attention to what they **sense**, **feel**, and **think** as they read and contemplate the scripture. Imaginative Prayer, and other contemplative practices like it, offer a powerful, fully embodied knowing of God and the Bible, tapping into our God-given authority and agency.[71]

In addition to using Imaginative Prayer when reading gospel scenes, Ignatius also invited participants to utilize their imagery mode during prayer time by imagining the face of God and noticing how God looked at them.[72] What a powerful, and revealing practice: *What does God's face look like when looking at me?*

In many ways, Ignatius was way ahead of his time. He knew from his own experience how transformative these practices were, but didn't have the research we do today on how the brain works, and how change and transformation take place in the body. We have often been taught in religious spaces that our spiritual formation and relationship with God is the outcome of some mix of the Spirit and our personal will at work, but in truth "attachment is the strongest force in the human brain."[73] As it pertains to the content of this chapter, what this means is that no amount of information about God will impact me positively if I don't have a healthy attachment to God.

But how is healthy attachment cultivated?

According to Neuroscientist Dr. Alan Schore, attachment is developed through joy, and joy is registered in the brain when we can tell that someone is genuinely glad to be with us.[74]

Joy is not something I simply think about and therefore have, I "know" it through my sensing and feeling in response to human relationships. This is where the genius of Ignatius comes in. I may not be able to have physical contact with God-made-manifest in the person of Jesus, but I can interact with him by utilizing my imagination and literally rewiring neural pathways as I do. I can envision what God's face looks like as God looks at me. And here's the thing—the way God's face looks at me, and at you, is the kind of look that registers joy in the brain. God is genuinely happy to be with us. In knowing this through sensing and feeling, as we engage imagery, we can build a healthy attachment to God, creating a fully embodied relationship with the Divine.

There was a season where the story of the Prodigal Son was deeply healing for me. I was identifying core wounds for the first time, noticing a particular tenderness that would rise up when I sensed someone important withdrawing and/or emotionally moving away from me. I needed to know I was loved and worth moving toward. And so, engaging in Imaginative Prayer, I would sit and close my eyes and envision myself in the scene:

> I am the prodigal son returning home. Somehow, even though I am still a far distance out, my Father sees me - as if he was just waiting there, looking intently for me. The moment he notices me he begins running. There is nothing calm, cool or collected about the ways he runs toward me. He is booking it, tears in his eyes, arms wide open. He reaches me, and embraces me as I fall into his arms.

In my imagination I would stay for a moment, allowing myself to joyfully take in the look on his face. He was so genuinely happy to see me. I allowed myself to receive his pursuit, and felt in my body the sensation of being held, known, loved. And as I did, I strengthened my embodied belief in my own belovedness: I am worthy of being moved toward.

Using Biblical Imagery to Reimagine God

I know I'm not alone in having transformative experiences of knowing God as a good Father, but what about God as a good Mother? How does the idea of a feminine God hit you? As I started to use Imaginative Prayer and build my healthy attachment with God, I started to explore some of these questions, and reassess my understanding of God.

We have no problems using male pronouns for God, but the moment someone refers to God as *She* or *Her,* people start squirming. Here are two common responses I've noticed to female pronouns for God: we either feel triggered, and then shut down the possibility without getting curious about what's just below the surface and *why* we feel the way we do (this was me for a long time), or we are intrigued but assume that any exploration of a feminine God will have to happen outside of the Bible and Christian circles. Both of these responses miss two really important biblical truths: God is not actually male or female because "God is not human," and the Bible contains both masculine and feminine imagery of God.[75]

God is a loving Father who sees me from a distance and runs to me. Equally as important and powerful, God is a tender Mother who, when the world becomes too big for me to solve, securely holds me in Her arms as I "calm and quiet myself" (Ps. 131:1-2). When I feel forgotten or overlooked, I am reminded that God, like a nursing Mother, offers Her very body to me and has even tattooed my name on Her hands (Isa. 49:14-16).

One of my most prized possessions is a spiral-bound workbook titled *Called Into Her Presence: Praying With Feminine Images of God* by Virginia Ann Frehle, R.S.M. I can't remember how I came across it or what inspired me to buy it, but its contents have become like water in a dessert I had no idea I was in. According to Frehle:

God is spirit. God is neither male or female—any more than

God is fire, rock, shepherd, shield, wind, king, light, or any other image we project. The images we choose for God, however, affect our relationship with God. They modify our view of ourselves and others. They even affect our political, social, and economic systems. The God-images we inherit and those we choose to use in prayer shape our lives.[76]

As women, we will struggle to fully claim ourselves if we cannot find ourselves reflected in the fullness of God. We have work to do in sorting through the image of "God the Father" we have been given that—*in reality*—may be little more than a patriarchal father figure. Any image of God as Father that does not have the expansiveness to include God as Mother is a false and incomplete image of God, because it does not reflect the full picture of God that we are given in Scripture. I was very intentional to title this section "Using Biblical Imagery To Reimagine God" because that is exactly what feminine imagery of God is: *biblical*. If this is the case, why do we keep telling the same old and incomplete story? A faith environment that is truly pro-women will acknowledge this formational reality, and will proactively find ways to not only invite women into the story, but show them they are already there.

Finding Myself In The Story Of The Dying Girl and Bleeding Woman

Several years ago, I began to bleed irregularly. To be honest, my periods had always been a bit unpredictable and so I didn't think much of it. I visited my gynecologist at the suggestion of a friend, assuming it was nothing. During an ultrasound my normally *very* upbeat doctor began to work to control her facial expressions, and her tone turned serious. She suggested a biopsy and told me to find a time to come back when my husband could join me.[77]

Left only to my imagination and Google, those weeks of waiting had me a bit anxious. When we don't know where our own stories are headed, there can be something therapeutic about finding our stories in another. I had been working my way through the Gospel of Mark, practicing Imaginative Prayer. When a particular story seemed to stir something in me, I would linger in it for a while. I was intentionally slow and attentive, and instead of studying the stories I was inviting them to study me.

When I came across the bleeding woman in Mark 5 my body told me to stay for a while. It's like I invited the woman to coffee and asked that she tell me her story over and over. Putting myself in her shoes, I soaked in each and every word, noticing when a particular detail stood out and stirred something up in me. I empathized with her suffering, even as she empathized with mine.

Over several weeks, months and now years, this woman, as well as the little dying girl whose story bookends the woman's, would become two of my closest companions. They have revealed parts of me left unclaimed. They have illuminated the ways in which women tend to stay asleep, play it small, and live as if invisible. They have invited me into my own embodied knowing and challenged me to act on my God-given authority and agency. They helped me to see how Jesus affirms, and even blesses, the disruption that comes when women move into their full humanity. Ultimately, they have been guides in my own female spiritual journey, extending the invitation they received from Jesus on to me: to Wake Up, Stand Up, and Come Out of Hiding.

This invitation is yours too.

In the coming chapters, I expand on the story of the Dying Girl and Bleeding Woman, and ask you to step into it yourself as we explore often overlooked details, practice Imaginative Prayer, and allow the story to be exactly what it is—disruptive to patriarchy and empowering for women.

The journey of becoming most fully human—most fully who God created us to be—is one that invites the whole self, in movement towards a whole God. Believe it or not, this whole female self and whole feminine God are both reflected in the pages of Scripture.

Dear reader, there is more for us. *So much more.* God and the Bible are ours to explore, to interpret, and to find ourselves in.

FOR FURTHER REFLECTION:

1. After finishing the chapter, take a few moments to be still and pay attention to what is stirring in you. What do you feel in your body? What emotions arise? Do you feel resistance of any kind? You don't need to solve anything. The invitation is to simply practice awareness, and to begin listening to your own embodied knowing.

2. As mentioned in this chapter, St. Ignatius of Loyola would invite people to consider the question: *What does God's face look like when looking at me?* Find a quiet space and close your eyes. Imagine God's face. What does God's face look like? And how is it that God looks at you? Imagine God's genuine gladness to be with you and allow yourself to receive this joy. Notice if you feel resistance, or if this is hard to do for any reason. Take some time to journal through the experience. Ask God for greater awareness of Divine presence with you, and for the ability to receive God's genuine gladness to be with you.

3. What stirs in you as you consider the idea of God as Mother? Consider how you have personally been impacted by the God images you have been given.

CHAPTER FIVE

THE STORY WITHIN A STORY

THE DYING GIRL AND BLEEDING WOMAN

When Jesus had again crossed over by boat to the other side of the lake, a large crowd gathered around him while he was by the lake. Then one of the synagogue leaders, named Jairus, came, and when he saw Jesus, he fell at his feet. He pleaded earnestly with him, "My little daughter is dying. Please come and put your hands on her so that she will be healed and live." So Jesus went with him.

A large crowd followed and pressed around him. And a woman was there who had been subject to bleeding for twelve years. She had suffered a great deal under the care of many doctors and had spent all she had, yet instead of getting better she grew worse. When she heard about Jesus, she came up behind him in the crowd and touched his cloak, because she thought, "If I just touch his clothes, I will be healed." Immediately her bleeding stopped and she felt in her body that she was freed from her suffering.

At once Jesus realized that power had gone out from him. He turned around in the crowd and asked, "Who touched my clothes?"

"You see the people crowding against you," his disciples answered, "and yet you can ask, 'Who touched me?'"

But Jesus kept looking around to see who had done it. Then the woman, knowing what had happened to her, came and fell at his feet and, trembling with fear, told him the whole truth. He said to her, "Daughter, your faith has healed you. Go in peace and be freed from your suffering."

While Jesus was still speaking, some people came from the house of Jairus, the synagogue leader. "Your daughter is dead," they said. "Why bother the teacher anymore?"

Overhearing what they said, Jesus told him, "Don't be afraid; just believe."

He did not let anyone follow him except Peter, James and John the brother of James. When they came to the home of the synagogue leader, Jesus saw a commotion, with people crying and wailing loudly. He went in and said to them, "Why all this commotion and wailing? The child is not dead but asleep." But they laughed at him.

After he put them all out, he took the child's father and mother and the disciples who were with him, and went in where the child was. He took her by the hand and said to her, "Talitha koum!" (which means "Little girl, I say to you, get up!"). Immediately the girl stood up and began to walk around (she was twelve years old). At this they were completely astonished. He gave strict orders not to let anyone know about this, and told them to give her something to eat. (Mark 5:21-43)

I affectionately call the above passage "the story within a story," which feels appropriate since it describes much of women's lives. Too often we are living a culturally appropriate life while unclaimed and forgotten parts of ourselves are just waiting to Wake Up, Stand Up, and Come Out of Hiding. And this is exactly, as I see it, what Jesus invites these women—and us—into.

The stories of the Dying Girl and the Bleeding Woman can be found in all three of the Synoptic Gospels—Matthew, Mark, and Luke.[78] These three books of the New Testament are linked because they share many of the same stories, and can be read and studied together (syn-optic means "see together")[79]. Scholars have long recognized that the accounts found in Matthew and Luke derive from Mark, meaning Mark was written first and then used as a source for the other two. In each of these accounts, the stories of the Dying Girl and Bleeding Woman are found together in what's known as an intercalation, or a sandwich narrative. An intercalation is used to weave two seemingly separate stories together, allowing them to enter into a vivid dialogue with one another. Maybe you already noticed how there are several overlapping elements in these stories:

- Two females in seemingly hopeless situations
- Desperation and courage in seeking Jesus for healing
- A woman and a girl who were considered ceremonially unclean, and Jesus, in making contact with them, would have then also been considered unclean
- The number twelve: the age of the girl and the number of years this woman had been bleeding
- The falling at the feet of Jesus, both by a man with power and by a woman without
- Both of these nameless females are referred to as "Daughter"
- The use of touch: the Bleeding Woman touches Jesus to be healed, and Jesus touches and takes the hand of the Dying Girl to heal her
- The role of faith in healing: Jesus says to the girl's father, "Don't be afraid; just believe," and to the bleeding woman, "Your faith has healed you"

- Both are restored, physically and presumably, to their places of belonging

These stories are more than just two incidents that happened alongside each other. They are meant to be explored together—meaning derived from one another. I have come to view this sandwich narrative as an *archetype*, containing a profound invitation for women and our spiritual development.

Archetype

An archetype is simply a universal pattern or prototype. Coined by Carl Jung, the term "archetype" represents "the patterns and possibilities of being human."[80]

Examples of popular archetypes include the nine Enneagram types, or the Hero's Journey, which many well-known stories have been modeled after. Lest you think that it is somehow inappropriate to pull archetypes out of Scripture, consider how we already do this. We find ourselves in the story of the Prodigal Son—are you the younger or older brother? Or how about Egypt, the Wilderness, and the Promised Land as stages in the spiritual journey? And almost every woman has been given the Mary and Martha archetypes—are you more of a sit at the feet of Jesus kind of gal, or a scurry around serving Jesus and wondering why no one is helping you kind of gal?

An archetype serves to help us make sense of our human experience. Within its universal pattern we find ourselves. Mysteriously, it creates space for our one-in-a-billion uniqueness, while also showing us how our experiences mirror one another. We are all different, and yet, we are very much the same.

A Female Journey Archetype

In the first chapter, I introduced one possible framework for the female spiritual journey. I suggested that the male-centered model women have largely been given—one that assumes a need to come face-to-face with our limits, surrender to a higher power, and take a journey of descent—is, in fact, a journey most women prematurely embarked on. As women in a patriarchal world, we have followed the message, "you must be less than you actually are," accepting our perceived limits as we surrendered ourselves to the higher power of patriarchy, usually starting at a young age. We have been on a journey of descent from the start.

Instead, a woman's journey toward being exactly human-sized will include coming face-to-face with her buried potentials, reclaiming what she surrendered (her/the self) to the god of patriarchy, and taking a journey of ascent. I believe that this very invitation is reflected in the archetype found in the Dying Girl and Bleeding Woman. Let's look again at the story, this time noticing how this invitation for women is present in the text.

The Dying Girl and Bleeding Woman (Bekah's Version)[81]

One day, as a large crowd gathered around Jesus, one of the synagogue leaders came, fell at his feet, and pleaded with him to come and heal his dying daughter. She was his only daughter and around 12-years-old. Jesus agreed, and he and his disciples went with him. They made their way through the crushing crowd—a crowd that included a woman who had been bleeding for twelve years.

Now, let's be clear. This "bleeding" is likely not about some kind of open wound and a problem with blood clotting. This is menstrual bleeding. This woman was going on twelve years of a nonstop period. She had sought the help of doctors and had spent all she had, but instead of getting better, she grew worse.

This was a complicated situation to be in, especially for a woman in biblical times. Perhaps the most difficult part would have been living with the label and stigma that came with menstrual bleeding: she was considered unclean (Lev. 15:25-27). According to the Jewish Law, anything or anyone she touched would also be deemed unclean for the rest of the day. In her condition, she was not allowed to go to the temple or synagogue, and was typically sequestered to a room. Others would have avoided all physical contact with her and anything she touched. This was a kind of social death.[82] She should not have been in that crowd, pressing up against and touching so many. There was a clearly defined place and path for her, and she was expected to stick to it.

But she had heard about Jesus and her intuition stirred, "If I just touch his clothes, I will be healed." The wise collaboration of her sensing, feeling, imagery, and thinking gave her the audacity to believe that maybe there was another way, *a different way*, to seek her healing. And so, trusting her own deep knowing, she made her way through this crushing crowd, spreading her label of "unclean" to each body she rubbed up against. Anemic from her condition, she would have been completely depleted from making her way through the crowd. Once close, she used what little energy remained to reach out her hand and touch Jesus' cloak.

The very thing she was forbidden to do—to touch—became her healing mechanism.

Immediately, her bleeding stopped, and she could feel in her body that she was free from her suffering. If this isn't astounding enough, what Mark tells us next is downright disturbing: "At once Jesus realized that power had gone out from him. He turned around in the crowd and asked, 'Who touched my clothes?'" Apparently, it wasn't a conscious choice for him to heal her. He turns, looking for who it is that *took his power*.

She took his power. (Chutzpah!)

Then the woman, knowing what had happened to her, came and fell at his feet and, trembling with fear, told him the whole truth. Everything. All of it. Her whole story. Including the part where she had just made Jesus unclean—*how would he respond to this?*

Jesus looks at the woman and rather than condemning her for such a brazen move, he blesses and affirms her by saying, "Daughter, YOUR faith has healed you. Go in peace and be freed from your suffering." This woman boldly made the move to come out of hiding, disrupting the system and taking Jesus's power without permission, and in doing so, both her physical and communal health were restored.

While Jesus spoke words of blessing and affirmation over this woman, the news comes that the little girl who he was on his way to help has died. Overhearing this, Jesus tells the girl's father, "Don't be afraid; just believe." And they continued on their way.

When they arrived at the house, they were met by people crying and wailing loudly. They had begun to mourn the death of this little girl. Jesus sees this happening, and in what could feel like a stunning lack of compassion, he asked: "Why all this commotion and wailing? The girl is not dead, but asleep." In response, the people laughed at him. I mean, what a ridiculous thing to say, right? But Jesus said it:

The girl is not dead, but asleep.

After this, Jesus, taking Peter, James, and John with him, went into the room where the girl and her parents were. He took her hand, and said to her: *"Girl, stand up!"* Immediately, she stood up and began walking around, leaving everybody astonished. Jesus gave strict orders to not mention what had happened, and told them to give the girl something to eat.

A Sandwich To Sink Your Teeth Into

When we consider this narrative sandwich, the meat—the middle part about the Bleeding Woman—is mind-blowing and disturbing. And the bread—the part about the Dying Girl—is just sort of bizarre. What happens when we allow these two stories to engage in vivid dialogue? How might they fit together?

What if the story of these two nameless females is really the story of all of us? A universal invitation from Jesus to walk our uniquely female path? Our ability as adult women to act with the authority and agency of the Bleeding Woman—practicing an audacious faith, that doesn't wait for permission and has the courage to disrupt the status quo—is inextricably linked to the Dying Girl in each of us being invited to wake up and stand up. To move into our full humanity as women will require us to go back and reclaim our seemingly lost and dead parts, and begin a journey of ascent as we step back into the fullness of who we are.

The Significance of Twelve

In Jewish culture, twelve traditionally represents the age when a girl becomes an adult (boys at thirteen). A bar or bat mitzvah are ceremonies which formalize and celebrate the individual's place in the adult Jewish community. The girl in the story, then, is dying at the very age she should be released from the control of her father, and launched into adulthood.

The term *patriarchy* in the Greek literally means "the rule of the father."[83] Additionally, in Scripture, the number twelve is thought to be symbolic of God's power and authority and also represents the perfection of God's government or rule.[84]

Twelve: A girl becomes an adult.

Twelve: Power, authority and government as designed by God.

What happens to a girl turning twelve, the age of adulthood, when the power, authority, and government in her world is not God-designed, but instead patriarchal? How does this inhibit her movement into adulthood? In "father rule" (patriarchy) a girl must stay functioning in the role of a daughter, even as an adult. The parts of her that are deemed unacceptable must die, or so it seems. Even the community around her assumes these parts dead (like the mourners in the story of the Dying Girl), moving ahead with their mourning rituals. Everyone moves on, making the necessary accommodations, and are disrupted when someone suggests otherwise.

Around 12-years-old is a time of significant change for a girl. Obviously, it's a time when puberty kicks in and the physical body begins to make the move from childhood to adulthood. Adolescence refers to "the social and personal experience of that process."[85] It's often a time of mixed messages, where a girl must attempt to reconcile her changing body with the culture's growing messages surrounding her appearance and place in culture: "Be beautiful, but beauty is only skin deep. Be sexy, but not sexual. Be honest, but don't hurt anyone's feelings. Be independent, but be nice. Be smart, but not so smart that you threaten boys."[86]

I was recently having coffee with a friend who shared how, at 12, she was competing in a spelling bee. She was doing well, but this presented a problem. She wanted to be (and was) smart, but felt that she must be careful with how she was perceived compared to her male classmates. She needed to be smart, but not *too* smart. She made the choice to purposely misspell a word, and a boy won the contest. My response to her story was a deep, deep resonance. Even though it may be hard to explain, I knew exactly why she did what she did. *All women do.* We learn, from a young age, that we must change ourselves to keep things peaceful. To fit the expected mold set out for us.

Carol Gilligan was one of the first female psychologists to study adolescent girls. Her work in the late 80s and early 90s revealed that significant shifts—beyond just the physical—happen for girls in this season of their lives, around 12 years old.[87] Referring to this research, Sue Monk Kidd describes what happens to an adolescent girl:

They undergo a gradual change in which they lose their feisty spirit, courage, and willingness to speak out—qualities they had known in girlhood. Around this time their truth becomes silenced, held back. They become afraid of conflict with males because they know on some level that males hold the power. They become—perhaps forever—good little girls, settling into the cliches and limits imposed on their gender.

So sleep begins. For some it can extend throughout life as unconsciousness deepens and numbness sets in. These women lose all memory of the problem they once saw. For other women the sleep is more fitful; they sometimes glimpse the truth, but it never seems to rouse them fully. These women tend to fall back asleep when the waking state becomes threatening (emphasis mine).[88]

French writer and feminist activist, Simone de Beauvoir described the adolescent shift for girls in this way:

Girls who were the subjects of their own lives became the objects of others' lives. [De Beauvoir] wrote, **"Young girls slowly bury their childhood,** put away their independent and imperious selves and submissively enter adult experience."** Adolescent girls experience a conflict between their status as human beings and their vocation as females. De Beauvoir said, "Girls stop being and start seeming" (emphasis mine).[89]

She's not dead,

but asleep.

How does a girl survive this impossible adolescent reality of being told she can't actually be who she is? She surrenders (albeit unconsciously) to the prevailing higher power. And she falls asleep.

Climb Out of Your Coffins: A Woman's Resistance to Waking Up

Wake up from your sleep,

Climb out of your coffins;

Christ will show you the light! (Eph. 5:14 MSG)

Ephesians 5 begins with this exhortation: "Follow God's example, therefore, as dearly loved children and walk in the way of love, just as Christ loved us and gave himself up for us as a fragrant offering and sacrifice to God" (Eph. 5:1-2). What better way to follow God's example, and walk in the way of love, than to imitate Jesus' resurrection by waking up and climbing out of our coffins?

Easier said than done.

As previously mentioned, adolescence only solidifies an already engrained reality for a girl—parts of her must "die" in order to be acceptable. By adulthood, women are well practiced at keeping whole parts of themselves buried and asleep. And so, when it comes to imitating Jesus, women are much better at the dying part than the rising part. In *Men and Women: The Journey of Spiritual Transformation*, Richard Rohr points out that in the gospel accounts, it is the men who need convincing of the cross, and the women who need convincing of the resurrection.[90]

I see his point—as women we have more than heeded Jesus' command to deny ourselves and take up our cross (Matt. 16:24). What we have actually denied is our very humanity, buying into a lie that it is our duty to be less than who we were created to be. *And this is sin.*

Imagine what it's really like for a man to be confronted with his limits. After being told all his life that he must be more than he actually is—that he should be big and powerful—he comes face-to-face with a harsh reality. He is not, and cannot be, those things. Will he accept this truth? Will he confess his complicity in attempting to be more than human-sized? The crucifixion is incredibly good, but hard news for him.

Why would we expect something different for a woman when confronted with her potential? After being told all her life that she must be less than she actually is—that she should be small and compliant—she comes face-to-face with a disorienting reality. She is, and always has been, much more than those things. Will she accept this truth? Will she confess her complicity in attempting to be less than human-sized? The resurrection is incredibly good, but uncomfortable news for her.

Women must make the choice: either accept or deny what they have been awakened to. Accepting will mean confession and repentance. Confess: name the truth of her premature surrender to patriarchy and admit her complicity in staying small. Repent: turn away from the god-like status she has given patriarchy and move in the direction of her full humanity, reflected in the One True God.

The alternative: deny the truth and fall back asleep.

Your Mission, Should You Choose to Accept It

The work of waking up and standing up are inextricably linked to the act of coming out of hiding. I'm not convinced that any of this works in some linear or formulaic fashion. One part doesn't necessarily come before another. The only thing I can say for sure is that this will stretch you. Literally. After a lifetime of playing it small, it is now time to expand. Stepping into your full humanity is going to ask you to get big (not bigger than human-sized, just bigger than you're used to). As a result, this journey is inevitably extremely disruptive. The world around you has grown accustomed to you being smaller than your fully, God-ordained size. Not unlike the bleeding woman who worked her way through the crowd, rubbing up against all the people and making them unclean in the process, as you begin to grow, you will find yourself rubbing up against people, ideas, systems, etc. And you'll know, because those people, ideas, systems, etc. will react.

It's like being the first to create boundaries in a family system. Although you are pursuing health, your boundaries will ask everyone to change. *And people don't like to change.* This process will take time, persistence, and lots of self-care.

Your mission, should you choose to accept it: honestly face your buried potential, reclaim what you have surrendered to the god of patriarchy, and begin the journey of ascent, courageously taking up all the space that was designated yours from eternity. In other words, Wake Up, Stand Up, and Come Out of Hiding.

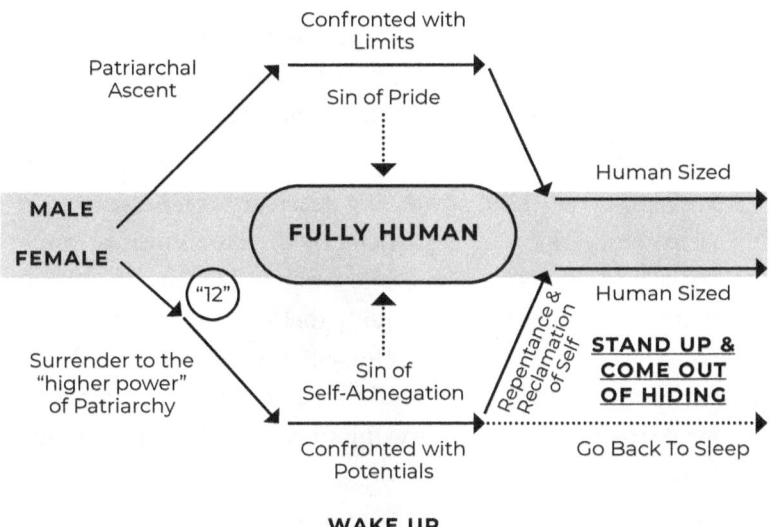

A Note on Being White, Privilege and Staying Asleep

A quick Google search on the internet is telling me there are multiple stages to sleep. I'm no expert on the subject, but I do resonate with the fact that some stages of sleep are deeper than others.

When it comes to my own physical well-being, I praise Jesus for a good night's rest (and for less appearance of bags under my eyes). However, when it comes to the kind of sleep I explore in this book, I feel a need to express caution, and name a hard truth about the "privilege" of being in deep, deep sleep.

As I mentioned in Chapter One, when we begin with a scarce narrative we end up with hierarchy. The world we inhabit is one where some have less and some have more—more money, more power, more influence, more options, more respect, and more favor. Those who have more power due to this hierarchy live with privilege, and one's ability to stay asleep usually correlates with their privilege. The same can be said for one's ability to fall back asleep if they find that being awake is too painful. Waking up rubs against our comfort and the "safety" of staying small. It means more responsibility, more knowledge, and potentially more disappointment as you become aware of patriarchal realities, including how others in your life may have encouraged your sleep, and might be unhappy if you awaken.

All this to say, any kind of warning necessary as it pertains to being asleep and waking up is particularly directed towards women with privilege—in particular, white women like myself. Alternatively, any kind of nuance—the reality that waking up may not be a choice, may happen much earlier for some, and that the movement toward being exactly human-sized might be resisted in more powerful and destructive ways—is primarily directed towards women of color.

Whoever you are, I hope you feel freedom to use this imagery of waking and sleeping (and the female spiritual journey framework) in ways that make sense with your unique circumstances. If you are white, like me, I hope you will recognize the great responsibility you have in how you manage your sleep. Our sleep not only keeps us numb—it is also the space in which "prophetic torpor" grows. This term, "prophetic torpor," was coined by Carol Lakey Hess to mean "the diminished capacity to care about and respond to injustice."[91] Hess argues that "self-abnegation blunts the person's prophetic and dissenting voice."[92] When we wake up, part of what we are waking up to is our voice, and our ability to use it for ourselves and others. We reclaim our capacity to be truth-tellers, offering what we can uniquely see, and naming it with authority. As white women, we must carefully steward the reality that we have greater access to power and privilege than our sisters of color—which we can either use for good (as we wake up and claim our voice and encourage others to do the same), or for ill (as we easily escape back into sleep because we are too uncomfortable, and therefore forfeit our prophetic voice).

What's Coming

In the chapters ahead we will be working our way through the three parts of Jesus' invitation: Wake Up (Chapter Six), Stand Up (Chapter Seven), and Come Out of Hiding (Chapter Eight). In each chapter, I guide you through the practice of imaginative prayer, inviting you to find yourself in the story of the Dying Girl and Bleeding Woman. *You are the Dying Girl. You are the Bleeding Woman.* Additionally, I'll offer several symbols and themes that I see in the story—all potential fodder for our own lives as we assess where we currently are on the female spiritual journey, and step more fully into who God created us to be.

In the story of the Dying Girl and the Bleeding Woman, we find that the gospel is even better news than we previously thought. Jesus sees us, affirms our humanity, and invites us to rise up. If you are anything like me, this invitation is both invigorating and terrifying. Will we accept it? And if we do, how will the world respond when we truly, fully show up? I hope you'll find out.

FOR FURTHER REFLECTION:

1. After finishing the chapter, take a few moments to be still and pay attention to what is stirring in you. What do you feel in your body? What emotions arise? Do you feel resistance of any kind? You don't need to solve anything. The invitation is to simply practice awareness, and to begin listening to your own embodied knowing.

2. Read through the story of the Dying Girl and Bleeding Woman in Mark 5: 21-43. Journal about what you notice, and what stands out to you.

3. Assess your ability (privilege) to go back to sleep if waking up begins to feel too uncomfortable. Can you identify your coping mechanisms in response to discomfort? What are the ways in which you may be tempted to escape back into sleep?

CHAPTER SIX

WAKE UP

YOU'RE NOT DEAD—JUST ASLEEP

"For always, always, we are waking up and then waking up some more."
— Sue Monk Kidd[93]

"When sleeping women wake, mountains move."
— Chinese Proverb

I'M a mom of teenagers, which means I still sometimes serve as a human alarm clock. The process is always the same: turn on the hall light, turn off the fan, pull back the covers and say, "Good Morning!" This is never a pleasant interaction, because no one likes being woken up, *especially teenagers.* Waking up is a process. The best mornings are unhurried and gentle, with time to put good nourishment in our bodies as we start our day. Waking up in the female spiritual journey is no different. There is plenty about it that will be unpleasant. It will be exponentially harder if we don't allow ourselves time to adjust or skip listening to our bodies as they tell us what we need.

This chapter focuses on discovering Jesus' invitation to Wake Up. I invite you to start with the practice of Imaginative Prayer, finding yourself in the story of the Dying Girl and interacting with Jesus' proclamation over us, "She's not dead, just asleep." After that, I offer several themes and corresponding reflection questions for you to journal through. As you read and reflect, pay attention to how God might be revealing areas of your life that are being invited to Wake Up.

Imaginative Prayer: Wake Up (Mark 5:21-24, 35-40)

Below you will find directions for the practice of Imaginative Prayer, and the section of Scripture that corresponds with the chapter's invitation. If it feels helpful to you, grab a journal and pen and write down your responses as you read. If you prefer to be guided in the practice, head over to **BekahStewart.com/imaginative-prayer** and simply click play on the Chapter Six link.

- Find a quiet space and get comfortable. Become aware of God's presence with you.

- **Reading One:** Simply read the story.

- **Reading Two:** During the second reading, pay attention to more detail. What is the setting like? What time of day is it? What is the mood and atmosphere like? How do people interact with one another?

- **Reading Three:** During the third reading, find yourself in the scene. Who or what are you? Are you a person? An animal? A tree? What are you doing, thinking or feeling? Use your senses. What are the sounds and smells? What are the emotions that rise up in you or in others?

- **Reading Four:** During the final reading, experience the story as the little girl. You are the one who Jesus has come to heal. It is your father who has sought help. It is your community that wails and mourns for your "death." It is you who Jesus says is not dead, but asleep. When the reading ends, let the story continue to unfold within you, in your imagination, mind, and heart, as the little girl.

- **Consider:** What's stirring? Standing out? Sticking? Where do you find yourself lingering? Is there an invitation for you to sit with and live into? Bring all of this into conversation with God.

When Jesus had again crossed over by boat to the other side of the lake, a large crowd gathered around him while he was by the lake. Then one of the synagogue leaders, named Jairus, came, and when he saw Jesus, he fell at his feet. He pleaded earnestly with him, "My little daughter is dying. Please come and put your hands on her so that she will be healed and live." So Jesus went with him . . . While Jesus was still speaking, some people came from the house of Jairus, the synagogue leader. "Your daughter is dead," they said. "Why bother the teacher anymore?"

Overhearing what they said, Jesus told him, "Don't be afraid; just believe." He did not let anyone follow him except Peter, James and John the brother of James. When they came to the home of the synagogue leader, Jesus saw a commotion, with people crying and wailing loudly. He went in and said to them, "Why all this commotion and wailing? The child is not dead but asleep." But they laughed at him.

(Mark 5:21-24, 35-40)

Wake Up: Themes To Explore

Twelve

> *"Then a man named Jairus, a synagogue leader, came and*
> *fell at Jesus' feet, pleading with him to come to his house*
> *because his only daughter, **a girl of about twelve**, was dying."*
> (Luke 8:41-42)

In my early thirties, a respected mentor gave me a guidebook—a resource that asked me to explore my "spiritual autobiography."[94] It directed me to recall my origin story: my family, my birth story, and the story of my name.

Growing up there was one tale I heard repeatedly. My parents had every intention of naming me Rachel Lynn, but after a traumatic (near-death) birth experience, I came home as Rebekah Joy. The changing of my name felt a bit like a legend to me. It seemed as if my name was meant to be changed, and that God was behind it all. From the very beginning of my existence, God had declared, *"Fear not, for I have redeemed you; I have called you by name, you are mine"* (Isa. 43:1).

As I spent time recalling how the changing of my name and other family stories had shaped me, I began to have a recurring memory. A moment in my life I hadn't thought of for nearly twenty years suddenly came flooding back.

I was twelve. I stepped out of my mom's car, and up on the curb near the school gym where the list was posted. I remember walking excitedly over to take a look. I fully expected to see my name after tryouts for the junior high dance team. I scanned the list once. Twice. A third time. I'm not sure when exactly it clicked. I hadn't missed it. They had missed me. *My name was missing.* In the world of this particular 12-year-old girl, not making the team was a devastating blow—a reality that took three scans to even consider.

As a spiritual director, I've been trained to see a recurring memory like this as a sacred invitation. It's as if God was sending me a Paperless Post with an event titled: "Your Name — A Treasure Hunt. Let's dig!" What was the discovery to be made? What kinds of clues could I find? I examined the possibilities from every angle. I peppered my parents with questions. I spent time reading about Rebekah in the bible. I dug into the meaning of names, and this is where I hit the jackpot.

Rebekah: to tie firmly; to secure

Joy: a feeling of great pleasure and happiness

I wondered, *does this name represent me?* I journaled through the names I found myself living under instead: the names given to me over time, the ways I had been labeled, and how in response, I had abandoned my true name to be accepted. These labels seemed to culminate into two main categories: Insecure and Unenjoyed. I could see that I had created a whole persona to cope and survive—one who found a sense of security externally and did my best to make myself pleasant to others.

The resounding questions started: when did I move from being Rebekah Joy (Secure and Enjoyed) to a covered-up version of Insecure and Unenjoyed? Is that original girl lost? Is she dead?

I don't believe that not making the dance team was a major turning point, but rather a representation of a time in my life when things were shifting. I was an adolescent, faced with what it would mean to become a woman in our world. Not finding my name was like a metaphor for the tumultuous internal realities a girl faces as she contends with the box she is being asked to fit into. As it turns out, the real treasure hunt God was sending me on through this recurring memory was not just about my name, but about a reclamation of my whole God-designed Self.

Rebekah Joy was not dead. She wasn't lost. To survive the world she found herself contending with, she had simply fallen asleep.

It's undeniable. Adolescence is a time of tremendous change in a girl's life. Even if she could somehow shut off the entire outside world, her body alone would still require her to shift and make sense of all that is morphing within her. But she can't shut off the outside world. As a girl's very body asks her to move into wom-anhood, her external realities often make many confusing and restrictive demands. As mentioned in Chapter Three, research reflects the importance of this time in a girl's life and the ways in which it contributes to a split from her feminine nature, rooted in an imbalance of values in our culture.[95]

I don't necessarily think there is something magical in the num-ber twelve. You may or may not have had something significant happen in that exact year of your life. However, I do think what it represents—*adolescence*—is something every woman ought to revisit and consider. This time in our lives likely contains messages and experiences that led us to fall asleep.

FOR REFLECTION:

As you engage with the following prompts and questions, invite the Holy Spirit to help you see what is there to see. Lean into any particular memories, ideas, themes, or words that seem to surface. Be careful not to overthink it, or to discount your knowing.

- When you reflect on your adolescent years (around 12 years old, late elementary to middle school) are there important life events that stand out? In that season, what personal experi-ences may have contributed to your feminine wounding?

- What messages did you receive as a girl from church, school, home, work, and/or within the culture at large during this time?

Dead or Asleep?

*"The child is **not dead but asleep**."*

As a child, I wanted to be a teacher when I grew up. One Christmas I was elated to find a large chalkboard under the tree, allowing me to set up my pretend classroom. I've always loved learning and finding ways to use my words to help others learn and connect ideas. As I got older, the assumed role this gifting would have to fit in (classroom teacher) didn't align with other interests, gifts, and passions of mine. And so, I moved on to other areas of interest.

In high school and college, I considered transferring to private Christian schools because I longed for my education to include learning about God and the Bible. In my early 20s, I considered attending seminary but resisted because the programs I wanted to participate in didn't seem to have any "logical" outcomes in terms of roles that would make sense for me. What was the point of spending so much money and time on something that couldn't lead anywhere?

It wasn't until I found myself in a church context where women preached and served in leadership that something unlocked in me. Once I was in an environment where my gifting had a place to go, doors began opening without me trying. I was asked to lead in greater and greater ways, and I finally pursued seminary and the Christian education I had always wanted.

The first time I was asked to consider preaching, I simultaneously felt terror and exhilaration. Some part of me wanted to, while another part of me questioned if I could pull it off. I never set out to be a pastor, let alone a teaching pastor. And why would I? I didn't grow up seeing women on a church platform. And yet, here I was, presented with an opportunity to lean into my gifting and ultimately, to invite a sleeping part of me to wake up.

As mentioned in Chapter One, a unique part of the spiritual journey for women is coming face-to-face not with her limits (like in the male journey), but instead with the enormity of her potential that has been pushed underground and put to sleep. Much of my work with vocational coaching clients involves exploring these potentials by following the trajectory of their life events and remembering desires and longings from their past. Most women get stuck along the way because of some perceived limit or closed door. What they want doesn't fit into a box they have been given, and so they set it aside.

The work of sifting through our "not dead, but sleeping" parts will poke at every expectation of what a woman should be. Imposter syndrome will likely rear its ugly head. My husband's mentor used to say, "Humility is not thinking less of yourself. It's thinking rightly of yourself." For a woman, untangling the difference between thinking less and thinking rightly is a massive task in and of itself. But take heart and remember Jesus' shocking words to those who had already labeled the girl a goner: "She's not dead, but asleep."

FOR REFLECTION:

- Can you think of "waking moments"—times when you have been given glimpses of yourself and your left-behind longings? Times where your eyes were opened and it felt like you were seeing something again, for the "first time"?

- What has been called dead in you that is just asleep? Where are you numb? Playing small? Attempting to keep the peace to not disrupt?

- What did you dream about as a child? What did you dream of being or doing? Do you still hold any of those dreams?

- Who do you long to be? What do you long to do? And what exactly is holding you back?

- What would it mean for these sleeping parts of you to wake up?

The Scoffers/Status Quo Keepers

"When they came to the home of the synagogue leader, Jesus saw a commotion, with people crying and wailing loudly. He went in and said to them, 'Why all this commotion and wailing? The child is not dead but asleep.' **But they laughed at him.**"

In Jesus' day, it was common practice to hire professional mourners when someone died.[96] According to most sources, these mourners were primarily women as it was considered improper for a man to publicly express grief. Apparently, the number of mourners reflected the societal status of the family. When Jesus arrives on the scene, he finds the hired mourners wailing and crying loudly. In response to the commotion, Jesus tells them that the girl is not dead, but asleep. And their response: *laughter.* The Voice translation puts it this way, "The mourners laughed a horrible, bitter laugh and went back to their wailing" (Mark 5:40 TV). These women had a job to do, and Jesus was an absurd distraction.

But what if there was something else going on? I'm struck by a group of women in the Ancient Near East making money by using their "voice." *In Women & Power: A Manifesto,* author Mary Beard explains that in the ancient world, public speaking was an exclusively male endeavor: "Public speaking and oratory were not merely things that ancient women didn't do: they were exclusive practices and skills that defined masculinity as a gender."[97]

If public speaking—a must in the world of politics and power— was reserved for men, then perhaps professional mourning was a way in which women could hold some slice of power within that system. They couldn't use their voice in the same way a man could, but they *could* use their voice. In an inherently scarce, patriarchal system, when women find their way into places of power, they are reluctant to release. Maybe in response to Jesus what these women were saying was, *"Don't mess with what power we have."*

Men are not the only ones capable of being blinded by power and duped into believing that the way things are is the way things always have to be. As we all know, this behavior isn't reserved for the ancient world. On the female spiritual journey, a woman's awakening will find resistance in a number of places and people; and maybe most painfully, among other women. Discovering that something or someone is not dead, just asleep, messes with people's paradigms and patterns. It impacts their roles and rules. It asks them to *change.* And good little girls generally don't cause this kind of disruption. Oh, how truly courageous it is to explore the world of living awake! As we do, let's not be naive about what it will mean for ourselves and those around us.

FOR REFLECTION:

- Who expects you to stay "dead"? How do you know this? Has this been directly or passively communicated to you?

- Who, if you woke up, would be thrown off, disrupted, shaken, and perhaps even threatened?

- What systems, roles, or rules might be disrupted if you wake up?

- What might have to change if you respond to Jesus' invitation to wake up?

Don't Be Afraid, Just Believe

"While Jesus was still speaking, some people came from the house of Jairus, the synagogue leader. "Your daughter is dead," they said. "Why bother the teacher anymore?" Overhearing what they said, Jesus told him, 'Don't be afraid; just believe.'"

Have you ever really stopped to consider just how tender and attuned Jesus was when tending to the Dying Girl? Imagine for a moment that you are Jairus. Your daughter is at home dying and you have pleaded with Jesus to come and help. Filled with anxiety, and wishing Jesus would walk a little faster, you are overwhelmed by the crowds and annoyed by the delay from a bizarre interaction between Jesus and a woman. And then you see them: familiar faces walking towards you. Your heart drops into your stomach because you know what they are about to say. *"She's gone. Don't bother the teacher anymore."* Not only is it too late, but you have also missed your final moments with her, never getting to say goodbye. You are about to crumble to the ground when you hear Jesus tenderly say to you, *"Don't be afraid; just believe."*

Jesus was not the stoic figure we sometimes make him out to

be. He understood what it meant to be human, and one could argue that if Jesus was fully and perfectly human, he was the most emotionally intelligent person to ever walk the earth. Jesus sees you and has compassion for you. He is with you and for you. He knows your fears and the very real risks involved in your waking up. He understands just how vulnerable this all is for you. He recognizes your fear and lovingly whispers in your ear, *"Don't be afraid; just believe."*

FOR REFLECTION:

- What hopes stir up as you consider parts of you that are being invited to wake up?

- What fear surfaces?

- Does it bring up any sadness? What might need to be grieved?

- In what ways will choosing to believe (in who you were created to be and become) and live in alignment, require you to get uncomfortable?

- What is Jesus asking you to believe about him and his power, or about you and your power?

Collect Your Insights

Now go back and revisit all that you have journaled throughout this chapter. Pay attention to any patterns, themes, or repeated words. What nuggets of gold can you dig up, illuminating who you are and where God is inviting you to Wake Up? Identify 1-3 next steps and write them down.

A Blessing for Waking Up

As you end this chapter, I invite you to receive this blessing from the late Irish poet, John O'Donahue. Notice what words stick or stand out. Consider opening your palms, and reading these words out loud.

"For a New Beginning"

In out of the way places of the heart
Where your thoughts never think to wander
This beginning has been quietly forming
Waiting until you were ready to emerge.

For a long time it has watched your desire
Feeling the emptiness grow inside you
Noticing how you willed yourself on
Still unable to leave what you had outgrown.

It watched you play with the seduction of safety
And the grey promises that sameness whispered
Heard the waves of turmoil rise and relent
Wondered would you always live like this.

Then the delight, when your courage kindled,
And out you stepped onto new ground,
Your eyes young again with energy and dream
A path of plenitude opening before you.

Though your destination is not clear
You can trust the promise of this opening;
Unfurl yourself into the grace of beginning
That is one with your life's desire.

Awaken your spirit to adventure
Hold nothing back, learn to find ease in risk
Soon you will be home in a new rhythm
For your soul senses the world that awaits you.[98]

Amen.

CHAPTER SEVEN

STAND UP

TAKING UP SPACE

The habits that keep you
from yourself,
the misconceptions
others have of you,
the unquestioned limits
you have allowed,
the smallness you have
squeezed yourself into:
these are not
who you are.
— Jan Richardson, from "Blessing for Knowing"[99]

Y husband, Chad, had a mentor who used to always say to him, "Fill the space you take up." Chad is a tall, attractive guy (if I may say so). Oftentimes people—based on what they see—expect him to show up and confidently assert himself, probably due to his appearance. What I love about Chad is that he is humble, emotionally intelligent, and just doesn't have the macho guy vibe. For some people, these things about Chad feel like a contradiction. They expect him to show up and be "big," and when he isn't, people can get kind of weird, awkwardly trying to fill the space they expected him to. (I cannot tell you how many times people have said the most awkward things about his biceps, or how he looks.) His mentor's advice wasn't about convincing him to act like a "dude." Instead, he was inviting Chad to notice the space people automatically made for him and to steward it well.

If I were to rework this mentor's wise words for women I would say, "Fill the space *you were meant* to take up." This is a monumental task for women—to not only believe that God made us for more, but to actually, courageously step into it. For the most part, no one in a patriarchal world is expecting women to *fully* show up, and generally speaking, women don't like to make others feel uncomfortable. Responding to Jesus' invitation to Stand Up is most certainly an act of faith.

This chapter focuses on hearing Jesus say to us, *"Talitha Koum!"* (*Little Girl, I say to you, get up!*). Once again, I invite you to start with the practice of Imaginative Prayer, finding yourself in the story of the Dying Girl as Jesus takes you by the hand. After that, I offer several themes and corresponding reflection questions for you to journal through. As you read and reflect, pay attention to how God might be revealing ways in which you are being invited to Stand Up and fill the space you were always meant to take up.

Imaginative Prayer: Stand Up (Mark 5:38-43)

Below, you will find the directions for the practice, and the section of Scripture that corresponds with the chapter's invitation. If it feels helpful to you, grab a journal and pen and write down your responses. If you prefer to be guided in the practice, head over to **BekahStewart.com/imaginative-prayer** and simply click play on the Chapter Seven link.

- Find a quiet space and get comfortable. Become aware of God's presence with you.

- **Reading One:** Simply read the story.

- **Reading Two:** During the second reading, pay attention to more detail. What is the setting like? What time of day is it? What is the mood and atmosphere like? How do people interact with one another?

- **Reading Three:** During the third reading, find yourself in the scene. Who or what are you? Are you a particular person? What are you doing, thinking or feeling? Use your senses. What are the sounds and smells? What are the emotions that rise up in you or in others?

- **Reading Four:** During the final reading, experience the story as the Little Girl. You are the one who Jesus extends a hand to and invites to stand up. When the reading ends, let the story continue to unfold within you, in your imagination, mind and heart, as the little girl.

- **Consider:** What's stirring? Standing out? Sticking? Where do you find yourself lingering? Is there an invitation for you to sit with and live into? Bring all of this into conversation with God.

When they came to the home of the synagogue leader, Jesus saw a commotion, with people crying and wailing loudly. He went in and said to them, "Why all this commotion and wailing? The child is not dead but asleep." But they laughed at him.

After he put them all out, he took the child's father and mother and the disciples who were with him, and went in where the child was. He took her by the hand and said to her, "Talitha koum!" (which means "Little girl, I say to you, get up!"). Immediately the girl stood up and began to walk around (she was twelve years old). At this they were completely astonished. He gave strict orders not to let anyone know about this, and told them to give her something to eat.

(Mark 5:38-43)

Stand Up: Themes To Explore

Little Girl, Stand Up!

> *"He took her by the hand and said to her, 'Talitha koum!'*
> *(which means '**Little girl, I say to you, get up!**')."*

Every year, I lead a group of women through a soul care experience I created called "Girl Stand Up." Over nine months, I guide the participants to listen to their lives, name who they are, and locate themselves on the female spiritual journey. We explore much of the content found here, as they interact with Jesus' invitation to Wake Up, Stand Up, and Come Out of Hiding.

I've watched women do incredibly hard and courageous work, differentiating themselves in their jobs, romantic partnerships, and community, asking for what they want and need, and saying no to life's realities that inhibit their movement into full humanity. To truly explore standing up in a world that is used to you playing small has a way of shaking things up. Much of this work is painful and scary, but sometimes it's just plain delightful.

On the shelf in our hearth room sits a beautiful abstract painting—a piece entitled "Coming Home." The artist, my friend Shannon, almost discarded it, before letting it sit on her counter for months. Eventually, she picked it up and took another look. Adding a layer of circles brought it to life.

What makes this artwork even more meaningful is that Shannon was a participant in Girl Stand Up, who, before joining, had no idea she was an abstract painter. As Shannon began to become acquainted with her Wild Child, inviting unclaimed parts of herself to the table, she picked up Julia Cameron's classic book *The Artist's Way*.[100] She began a practice of stepping into and exploring this sleeping part of her. As a result, Shannon is now, quite literally, taking up space in the world as her artwork is displayed in homes around the country (and on the cover of this very book!).

Shannon named the piece "Coming Home" because in her words, "In this journey of being an emerging artist, I believe I am coming home to one of the sweetest parts of how my Creator made me." Adding circles brought the art piece to life, just as Shannon returning back to lost and hidden parts of herself created a full-circle moment in her own life.

In Chapter One and Chapter Five, I shared about the female spiritual journey, and how in response to being told, "You must become less than you actually are," women must contend with the sin of self-abnegation, or the renouncing and rejection of Self. Jesus' invitation to Stand Up is about stepping back into and reclaiming our full Self.

FOR REFLECTION:

- Can you name areas/parts of yourself that you have rejected, renounced, made small, been overly apologetic for, forgotten, etc.?

- If you are struggling to name these lost and hidden parts, consider revisiting your childhood dreams. When you were young, what did you enjoy? What jobs did you dream of one day having? What kinds of roles and realities filled your daydreams?

- Perhaps have a conversation with God about these areas, admitting your tendency to resist your full humanity, and asking for the grace to re-claim your full self.

Divine Urgency

"*Immediately the girl stood up and began to walk around.*"

There is something to be said for learning the art of waiting in a world of instant gratification, but let's not too quickly overlook the reality that for women, waiting has been engrained as a cultural value from the beginning. Women who move swiftly toward what they want and need are often interpreted as too much: too masculine, too brazen, too self-focused. The assumption is that a "good" woman (i.e. good female friend, mom, wife, sister, co-worker, etc.) will make sure everyone in her orbit is cared for before she tends to herself. She is patient and waits for the right moment, whether it ever comes or not. She ensures the mood is right and she won't disrupt anything prematurely.

In response to Jesus' invitation to Stand Up, the text communicates both immediacy and movement. At once the girl stands up and begins walking around. If Jesus invites us to Stand Up, the time is *now*. There are many factors that will lull us back to sleep, not least of which is the distraction of cultural expectations and norms.

If Jesus is telling you to Stand Up, I encourage you to listen and respond—with urgency.

FOR REFLECTION:

- What are you waiting on to Stand Up? What's keeping you stuck? Do you think you need someone to give you permission? And if so, who is that permission-giver? What is keeping you from moving toward what you want?

- How does fear create resistance as you consider standing up? What labels are you afraid of being given?

- As you consider the reflection questions from the previous section (what parts have you rejected, etc.), what might it look like for you to confidently, and with a sense of urgency, own these parts of yourself?

- In the next days, weeks, and months, what might movement look like? Is there a specific direction that the Spirit is inviting you to head in? How might you be intentional to respond in a fully embodied way, and not just via your Thinking mode of knowing?

Inviting Our Family of Origin Into the Room

> "*After he put them all out,* **he took the child's** **father and mother** *and the disciples who were with him, and went in where the child was.*"

For a season, I was seeing both a therapist and a spiritual director simultaneously. Both were helping me look lovingly at my childhood wounds, processing ways in which they still impacted me as an adult. Over time it became clear that there was one wound in particular that seemed to accompany me into adulthood. I would find myself in painful situations where this childhood wound was poked at, and although I might be reacting to the person from my adult world in real-time, the force with which my response came had more to do with that old unhealed wound.

When both my therapist and spiritual director separately encouraged me to work through and identify what exactly needed to be released and forgiven, I set aside time and reserved a room at my go-to retreat center to get curious about this wound. After several hours of journaling through tears, I was exhausted. All I wanted to do was sleep. And so, listening to my body, I set my journal aside and laid down. Coincidentally, this exploration of childhood wounds overlapped with the season I began to deep dive into the story of the Dying Girl and Bleeding Woman. As I laid down an idea came to me. I would allow my lying down to represent my release of these past wounds. I would sleep without an alarm, trusting God to wake me up when I was physically ready. And, upon waking, I would respond to Jesus' invitation to Stand Up, immediately rising from bed as an embodied way of trusting my ability to move forward, having let go of what needed to be released.

There was something deeply transformative about inviting my body into the process of responding to childhood wounds and trusting her to lead the way into Standing Up. Finding myself in the story of the Dying Girl allowed me to imaginatively include Jesus in my healing, as I faithfully responded to his invitation in the "presence" of my family of origin.

Each of our stories are unique, and some of us have an easier time remembering and accessing childhood wounds than others. No matter how stable or chaotic one's childhood experience is, no one escapes the reality that their family of origin has profoundly impacted them. One of the hardest things for someone hanging on to the good little girl mentality, and who grew up in a relatively good and safe home, is to admit that we *all* experience core wounds at a very early age. These core wounds significantly shape the trajectory of our lives. If you had a wonderful and stable upbringing, I encourage you to pause, give thanks, and then allow yourself permission to truly explore how those wonderful and stable adults shaped you.

In the journey of becoming fully human—most fully who God created us to be—the work of identifying and working through childhood wounds is non-negotiable. We must explore and name the realities of our childhood, seek to forgive and heal where we can, and then learn to parent ourselves via our Nurturing Parent sub-personality. This work will require the greatest of care as it will invite us into our most vulnerable and tender places. We will struggle if the parameters and/or environment do not feel gentle and safe. I believe that everyone will benefit from seasons of seeking out trusted guides who are professionally trained and can skillfully guide us. If that's not accessible to you at the moment, use the following questions to start your reflections and processing of childhood wounds.

FOR REFLECTION:

- In Chapter Three, under the section "Our Gift to Offer: Wounded Child and False Self," I shared that one of the most important questions I ask vocational coaching clients is the following: *What did you need (in childhood) that you did not receive?*[101] Is there any connection between your answer to this question and your ability to Stand Up? If your parents weren't able/aren't able to provide these needs, how else have you/will you meet them (in healthy ways) in order to fully Stand Up and reclaim the self?

• According to Carl Jung, "Nothing has a stronger influence psychologically on their environment and especially on their children than the unlived life of the parent."[102] Exactly how our family of origin impacted us can be hard to see and name. We don't always pay attention to the ways in which our caregivers' lives (or unlived lives) have indirectly influenced us, and we might not know what dreams our caretakers haven't realized. This might require you to do a little digging, but what unmet dreams did your parents or caregivers have? What is their backstory? What were their greatest influences? What were their greatest life inhibitors? What kinds of insights can you gather from this information for the areas you're being invited to Stand Up, and/or reasons why you resist?

• Can you think of scenarios, outside of your family, where you tend to stay small because a core childhood wounding is being reopened?

• Consider your Wounded Child. What is it like—during the practice of Imaginative Prayer—for her to have this interaction with Jesus? Perhaps return to the practice of Imaginative Prayer, but this time bring your Nurturing Parent along, allowing her to imitate Christ in offering a hand, inviting her to stand up, and directing her to be nourished.

• Invite your body into the healing process by creating a symbolic threshold experience. Take a nap or sleep for the night after completing the Imaginative Prayer exercise and reflection questions, and upon waking, allow yourself to respond to

Jesus' invitation to Stand Up. In the coming days and weeks, notice if you are responding differently to these wounds when they are poked at.

Take Care

> "*He gave strict orders not to let anyone know about this, and told them to* **give her something to eat.**"

There was a time when I would have read this seemingly random detail, when Jesus instructed them to give her something to eat and would forget it almost as soon as I was done reading it. Now I know better.

Although the work of standing up will ultimately bring freedom, the process will likely test you in every way. You will not survive this journey if you don't listen to and attune to your very real embodied needs. It may seem basic, but Jesus is concerned with whether or not you put good food in your body. Do you get good sleep? Do you set boundaries to protect your sanity? Do you seek healthy community? Do you take walks? Listen to good music? Do you allow yourself joy and delight?

Why risk everything to reclaim the self, if you aren't actually going to care for the self? And the moment you are tempted to buy into the lie that says listening to and attuning to your own needs is selfish, remember these wise words from Parker Palmer: "Self-Care is never a selfish act—it is simply good stewardship of the only gift I have, the gift I was put on earth to offer others. Anytime we can listen to true self and give it the care it requires, we do so not only for ourselves, but for the many others whose lives we touch."[103]

Take care of yourself, because what good is Standing Up if you don't have the energy to walk out of the room and into the life God intended for you to live?

FOR REFLECTION:

- What is your relationship to food? So many women (most of us?) have unhealthy and complicated ways in which we relate to food and why we eat (or don't). This is another one of those areas where we may need a season of seeking guidance from a trained guide (therapist, doctor, nutritionist, etc.).

- The work of standing up is courageous and hard work. It is exposing and vulnerable. What will you need in order to nourish your whole self so that you can Stand Up, and stay standing? Take time to consider each of the categories below. Listen and allow your embodied knowing to tell you what you long for and need. Beware of letting "should" take over here. Be intentional to tap into desire and true personal replenishment.

  - Physical
  - Intellectual
  - Emotional
  - Spiritual

Collect Your Insights

Now go back and revisit all that you have journaled for this chapter. Pay attention to any patterns, themes or repeated words. What nuggets of gold can you dig up, illuminating who you are and where God is inviting you to Stand Up? Identify 1-3 next steps and write them down.

A Blessing for Standing Up

As you end this chapter, I invite you to receive another one of my favorite blessings from the late Irish poet, John O'Donahue (yes, I am a big fan). Notice what words stick or stand out. Consider opening your palms, and reading these words out loud.

"For Presence"

> Awaken to the mystery of being here
> and enter the quiet immensity of your own presence.
> Have joy and peace in the temple of your senses.
> Receive great encouragement when new frontiers
> beckon.
> Respond to the call of your gift and the courage to
> follow its path.
> Let the flame of anger free you of all falsity.
> May warmth of heart keep your presence aflame.
> May anxiety never linger about you.
> May your outer dignity mirror an inner dignity of soul.
> Take time to celebrate the quiet miracles that seek no
> attention.
> Be consoled in the secret symmetry of your soul.
> May you experience each day as a sacred gift woven
> around the heart of wonder.[104]

Amen.

CHAPTER EIGHT

COME OUT OF HIDING

DISRUPTING THE STATUS QUO

Women, and others whose selves are in 'hiding,' need to claim their selves before God; leaders of women need to proclaim this side of the gospel news and promote the development of women's selves.

— Carol Lakey Hess[105]

Anger has been brewing in women for millennia. Of course it has. Who wouldn't be angry about being excluded, intimidated, mistrusted, belittled, accused, abused, raped, and a myriad of other means of repression? But since women have been told that anger is unbecoming, unfeminine, unacceptable, the anger went underground. Repressed anger is a dangerous thing.

— Elizabeth Lesser[106]

I was recently playing hide and seek with my daughter. I found an amazing hiding spot in the dark garage where I knew she would struggle to find me. I was right. After some considerable time had passed, the satisfaction of my ability to find the perfect spot began to rub up against the reality that by being in that spot, I was no longer enjoying the game. I wasn't enjoying *anything*. I was sitting in the dark, waiting for someone else to find me. Ironically, my daughter eventually moved on. Turns out the game was over, and I didn't even know it.

Patriarchy is like stepping into a big game of hide and seek, however, women are not allowed to be the seekers. That kind of role is meant for men who are apparently better equipped to do the finding, the hunting, the rescuing. Women become experts at staying hidden. We know the rules and we play by them, hoping that it won't take too long to be found. But what if it does take too long? When women begin to Wake Up to the patriarchy game, and the reality that we have handed over our agency, we must make a choice. Will we stay hidden? Or will we abruptly end the game by Coming Out of Hiding?

This chapter focuses on exploring the audacity of the Bleeding Woman, as she bravely came out of hiding. For a final time, I invite you to start with the practice of Imaginative Prayer, finding yourself in the story of the Bleeding Woman. After that, I offer several themes and corresponding reflection questions for you to journal through. As you read and reflect, pay attention to how God might be affirming the wisdom of your body, and blessing a potentially disruptive path toward your full humanity.

Imaginative Prayer: Come Out of Hiding (Mark 5:24-34)

Below you will find directions for the practice, and the section of Scripture that corresponds with the chapter's invitation. If it feels helpful to you, grab a journal and pen and write down your responses. If you prefer to be guided in the practice, head over to **BekahStewart.com/imaginative-prayer** and simply click play on the Chapter Eight link.

- Find a quiet space and get comfortable. Become aware of God's presence with you.

- **Reading One:** Simply read the story.

- **Reading Two:** During the second reading, pay attention to more detail. What is the setting like? What time of day is it?

What is the mood and atmosphere like? How do people interact with one another?

- **Reading Three:** During the third reading, find yourself in the scene. Who or what are you? Are you a person? What are you doing, thinking or feeling? Use your senses. What are the sounds and smells? What are the emotions that rise up in you or in others?

- **Reading Four:** During this final reading, I want you to experience the story as the bleeding woman. After 12 years of suffering, you are the one who boldly makes the move to come out of hiding, disrupting the system, and taking Jesus's power without permission. When the reading ends, let the story continue to unfold within you, in your imagination, mind and heart.

- **Consider:** What's stirring? Standing out? Sticking? Where do you find yourself lingering? Is there an invitation for you to sit with and live into? Bring all of this into conversation with God.

A large crowd followed and pressed around him. And a woman was there who had been subject to bleeding for twelve years. She had suffered a great deal under the care of many doctors and had spent all she had, yet instead of getting better she grew worse. When she heard about Jesus, she came up behind him in the crowd and touched his cloak, because she thought, "If I just touch his clothes, I will be healed." Immediately her bleeding stopped and she felt in her body that she was freed from her suffering.

At once Jesus realized that power had gone out from him. He turned around in the crowd and asked, "Who touched my clothes?"

"You see the people crowding against you," his disciples answered, "and yet you can ask, 'Who touched me?'"

But Jesus kept looking around to see who had done it. Then the woman, knowing what had happened to her, came and fell at his feet and, trembling with fear, told him the whole truth. He said to her, "Daughter, your faith has healed you. Go in peace and be freed from your suffering."

(Mark 5:24-34)

Come Out of Hiding: Themes to Explore

"Unclean": Labeled and left behind.

> *"And a woman was there who had been*
> ***subject to bleeding*** *for twelve years."*

I was first introduced to Rachel Held Evans through her book, *A Year of Biblical Womanhood*.[107] In it, Evans brilliantly exposes the ways in which biblical literalists turn out to be not-so-literal in their day-to-day interpretations of scripture. For a year, Rachel attempted to follow biblical guidelines for women. Any time she experienced menstrual bleeding, she removed herself from the community. She refrained from church, carried around a cushion at home so as to not make contact with anything she sat on, abstained from touching her husband and even slept in a tent! Rachel's experiment humorously revealed modern-day misses in biblical interpretation, but it also illuminated the very real barriers in place for a woman in the Bleeding Woman's situation. It's one thing to be considered unclean each month during your period. It's another thing to experience bleeding for twelve straight years.

As mentioned in Chapter Five, a status of "unclean" meant the Bleeding Woman wasn't allowed in the temple or synagogue, and was likely confined to one room at home. Hers was a life marked by isolation and loneliness as family and the community would have avoided all contact with her. The system labeled her a social outcast, and without effective medical care, she was seemingly powerless to do anything about it. She was labeled and left behind.

Times have changed . . . *mostly*. Women's labels today aren't always as overt, but make no mistake—they exist. If we are to imitate the audacious faith of the Bleeding Woman, we must face the labels we live under and that hold us back. The faith required to fully reclaim the self will mean granting ourselves permission to confront restrictive societal expectations, and believing it's possible (and even favorable to God) to find a new way.

FOR REFLECTION:

- What are the labels given to women in patriarchy in order to prop up the system and keep women small/in hiding? (Too much, emotionally out of control, too sensitive, weak, angry, dumb, flaky, irrational, a bitch. They could even be seemingly positive: nurturing, always invitational, and patient, for example.) How have these labels impacted you personally?

- Additionally, what are labels or restrictive expectations you've been given by your family of origin, or other life circumstances? (Don't get dirty, behave properly, be compliant, be quiet, be a "good little girl," etc.)

- Can you name ways in which these labels and expectations play out for you today? What is actively keeping you small and/or in hiding in important relationships, at work, etc.?

Un-pledging our Allegiance to Patriarchy

"A large crowd followed and pressed around him.
And a woman was there *who had been subject to bleeding . . . "*

It may not have been conscious, but for the Bleeding Woman to basically say, *"to hell with the labels and the system's rules"* by making her way through the crowd, and reaching out to touch Jesus meant that she shifted in her allegiance. For a time, she played by the rules, carefully obeying the guidelines given to her. But eventually, something changed. I wish we knew more about her thought process and all that was stirring and stewing inside. We can assume she was desperate after so many years of suffering, spending all she had to only get worse. This woman hit her breaking point and was no longer willing to sacrifice her own personhood for the sake of a system that could not support her full humanity.

In Chapter One, I described the female spiritual journey in this way:

She will come face-to-face, not with her limits—but instead—with the enormity of her potential that has been pushed underground and put to sleep. She must confess the god-like status she has given to patriarchy, and repent, which simply means to turn. She must head in a new direction—one that faces a God who is truly for her, reflects her full self, and invites her into the journey of becoming most fully who she was created to be. Now she can begin the journey of ascent, courageously taking up all the space that was designated hers from eternity.

Is this not a description of the Bleeding Woman's story? Painfully aware of the labels and limits given to her by a broken system, she was driven to her depths and confronted with her own worth as a human. It was here that she found the gumption to believe she was made for more than her current existence. It was this belief that compelled her to repent, which literally means to turn. She stopped placing her trust in the system, and instead turned toward the One True God, placing her faith in another Higher Power who would humanize and help her. She risked potential shame, ridicule, and embarrassment from her community because for a moment, she believed in herself, and the power of Jesus, more. Ultimately it was the result of her own potential—her inner knowing mixed with acting on a courageous faith—that propelled her forward.

What if our allegiance to God has been intermixed with allegiance to a god, such as a system, person, status quo, level of privilege, etc.? What if the image of "God the Father" we've been given and have surrendered to is actually little more than a patriarchal father figure? I realize this idea may be hard to stomach. The truth is, we all do this in various ways: we bring in distorted ideas of who or what God is. It's called idol worship. When we begin to see that our view of God is distorted, the appropriate response is to confess our error, and adjust our lives in order to re-align with the One True God. If there is any part of the god you are worshiping that

is not truly for you,

does not reflect your true Self,

or does not affirm a journey into your full dignified humanity

then you can be sure that there are some important issues to sort through, and some God-images to throw out.

FOR REFLECTION:

- How would you describe the "system" or institution from which you were first given your God-image?

- What are the unspoken rules you've been given as it pertains to being a woman of faith?

- When you honestly consider your loyalty, is it first to God or to the "system"? (If the system has told you it is equal with God, or in some way holds power that you don't—it's a sign of unhealth, FYI.)

- Is your God-Image 1) truly for you, 2) reflective of your full Self, and 3) affirming of your full dignified humanity?

- Are there areas or ways in which you have pledged allegiance to a system built around a god, but have called it allegiance to God? If so, I encourage you to have a conversation with the One True God about this. And as you do, remember that God is like a tender Mother. She loves you, welcomes you into her embrace, and delights in hearing from you.

Disrupting the Status Quo

"A large crowd followed and pressed around him.
And a woman was there who had been subject to bleeding . . . "

I'm always struck by how watered-down this story is told. Most people avoid speaking to the reality that this is a story about irregular **menstrual** bleeding (I dare you to find me a sermon where a male pastor mentions a period from the platform). This scene is described as if she meekly made her way through the crowd without being noticed and without a commotion.

I call bullshit.

This is not a nice, sweet story. There is nothing polite about it. The Bleeding Woman is everything a woman is not supposed to be. She was angry from all those years of feeling invisible. And rather than suppressing this un-ladylike emotion, she listened to it. She left the place she was supposed to stay, snubbed the system, broke the rules, pushed her way through a crowd of people, and made every single person she touched unclean in the process. Remember that Jesus was on his way to help someone else, but she didn't say, "I'll wait until it's my turn." She needed what she needed now, and she took it. Talk about a fiercely assertive woman who made a lot of people very uncomfortable.

This isn't to say that she felt no fear. I'm sure she was scared out of her mind. There were no guarantees. However, she didn't wait until she could be sure that everything would go perfectly, strategizing how to ruffle the least amount of feathers. She was risking it all and the chances it would turn out poorly were high—like, very high.

The Bleeding Woman's example reminds me of important words from American civil rights activist and icon John Lewis: "Never, ever be afraid to make some noise and get in good trouble, necessary trouble."[108]

FOR REFLECTION:

- When you consider your labels (from the section "Unclean: Labeled and Left Behind), what would it look like for you to push back and disrupt the status quo? What actions might this require? Who might be impacted/upset?

- What is your relationship to anger? What are your patterns in dealing with it when it arises? Do you understand anger to be good or bad? Positive or negative? Name a time you experienced both positive anger and negative anger. What might it look like for you to cultivate a healthy relationship with anger, listening for its wisdom and invitation?

- Is there a correlation between feeling invisible and hiding? Is it possible that areas in our lives in which we feel invisible are pointing to an opportunity to courageously come out of hiding? If so, where are feelings of invisibility in your own life offering an invitation to act courageously?

Let Your Life Speak

*". . . **she thought**, 'If I just touch his clothes, I will be healed.'*
*Immediately her bleeding stopped and **she felt in her body** that*
she was freed from her suffering."

I read a lot, but there are few books I read more than once, and really only one that I intentionally read every year. Parker Palmer's *Let Your Life Speak: Listening for the Voice of Vocation* is, in my opinion, required reading for every human. Palmer's words oozed wisdom as he insightfully wrote about the art of listening from within:

> Verbalizing is not the only way our lives speak, of course. They speak through our actions and reactions, our intuitions and instincts, our feelings and bodily states of being, perhaps more profoundly than through our words. We are

like plants, full of tropisms that draw us toward certain experiences and repel us from others. If we can learn to read our own responses to our own experience—a text we are writing unconsciously every day we spend on earth—we will receive the guidance we need to live more authentic lives.[109]

Our life constantly offers us clues about who we are and the life we were created for if only we would pay attention. The Bleeding Woman seemed to be well practiced in the art of listening to her life. The text tells us "She thought, 'If I just touch his clothes, I will be healed.'" She had likely heard about Jesus and the miracles he performed in healing others. Even though there was a clearly defined path for her and expectations for how she would handle her labels, she had a hunch that Jesus might open up a different possibility and she chose to listen to her intuition. Additionally, the Gospel of Mark tells us that after reaching out to touch Jesus, *"she felt in her body"* that she had been healed. This woman had a deep embodied knowing. She listened to her body and trusted what it was telling her.

Women, by design, are a powerhouse of embodied knowing, but this doesn't automatically mean we are attuned to our own deep well of insight. Listening to and honoring our lives takes practice, and will wane without intentionality. As Clarissa Pinkola Estés says:

I've heard women say it, if not a hundred times, then a thousand times: 'I knew I should have listened to my intuition. I sensed that I should/should not have done such and such, but I didn't listen.' We feed the deep intuitive self by listening to it and acting upon its advice. It is a personage in its own right, a magical dollish-sized being which inhabits the psychic land of the interior woman. In this way it is like a muscle in the body. If a muscle is not used, eventually it withers. Intuition is exactly like that: without food, without employment, it atrophies.[110]

We were designed on purpose by a Good Creator. It is possible to know ourselves and to live in alignment, but first we must learn to listen to and trust our own knowing.

FOR REFLECTION:

- How "at home in your skin" do you feel? How present? Rooted? Sensitive? Alive?

- Do you love your body? Do you feel comfortable in it? Do you trust it?

- Can you recognize your own embodied knowing, or "intuition"? Try and describe what it feels like in your body when you know that you know that you know.

- Can you think of a time where your body/intuition was trying to tell you something? Did you listen? How did you respond?

- What is a current rhythm in your life that is helping you listen to your life and grow in attunement with your body? If there isn't one, the practice of simple examen (introduced in the "For Further Reflection" section of Chapter Two) is a helpful tool to consider.

- Are there areas of your life currently where something is stirring and/or you sense a need to act? What's stopping you? Do you trust your body?

She Took His Power

*"At once **Jesus realized that power had gone out from him**.*
He turned around in the crowd and asked,
'Who touched my clothes?'"

I would love to see this part of the story depicted in a children's Bible. I mean, how do we really address what is happening without some squirming, a few disclaimers, and warnings about all the possible dangers inherent in following this woman's example? We just don't have a category for this kind of behavior, especially when the main character is a woman. I'm sure we could come up with ways to soften what is happening, but the bottom line is this: the Bleeding Woman seeks her healing through forbidden means (touch), and takes Jesus' power without permission.

Can you imagine all that was happening inside this woman as she touched Jesus? She exercised her God-given agency and authority (*empowerment!*), took Jesus' power, and was healed immediately (*shock and relief!*), and then seconds later, Jesus asked who touched him (*Oh shit!*). How would this God-man—whose power she just took without permission—respond when he realized it was an unclean outcast who touched him (*shame!*)? No wonder she fell at his feet, "trembling with fear." And then Jesus went and did a beautiful, Jesus-y thing. He saw her (*dignified!*), heard her whole story (*understood!*), affirmed her (*reassured!*), and blessed her journey forward (*commissioned with confidence!*).

The good news always turns out to be better than we thought, and more disruptive than what we're actually comfortable with (*hallelujah!*).

FOR REFLECTION:

- Where in your life are you waiting for permission from outside of you rather than exercising the God-given authority and agency within you? Who have you looked to as "permission givers"?

- What is your relationship to power? To authority? When have you felt truly empowered?

- What is one area of your life where you have handed power and authority over to others and actively need to take back ownership of?

- Is there a current circumstance where you are being invited to take action? To seek what you need or want without another's permission or stamp of approval?

Her Whole Truth

> *"Then the woman, knowing what had happened to her,*
> *came and fell at his feet and, trembling with fear,*
> ***told him the whole truth."***

I wonder where she started with her truth. From the very beginning? Perhaps from that time when she began to notice irregularities? Did she share feelings of abandonment, bouts of depression, and the millions of times she had cried out to God with seemingly no response? Did she speak of her suffering, and the doctors who took all her money? Did she explain her rationale, and how desperation drove her to break all the rules? Did her body shake and voice quake?

We don't know the intimate details of this exchange or how long it lasted, but we do know that she told Jesus her whole truth. She didn't sugarcoat or hold back. She offered him her whole story—she offered him her whole self.

Physical healing occurred when the woman touched Jesus, but her full reclamation of self was in process, and the moments after her physical healing were, in many ways, just as important. Telling her whole truth meant finding her voice, and allowing the details of her life to take up space and time in a crowded place, with important business to attend to.

To tell the truth of our lives—to ourselves, others, and God—is an act of faith. It is a proclamation that our story matters within the bigger story, putting our God-given agency on display. Cole Arthur Riley wrote so beautifully about this act of liberation:

Whenever I become uncertain of which direction liberation lies in, I ask myself to tell the truth. Not that I am capable of comprehending what any ultimate Truth is. But I am capable of at least telling the truth about what I believe to be true—my inmost convictions, desires, or even embodied revelation. The truth that rattles in my bones."[111]

FOR REFLECTION:

- What is the correlation between owning our God-given authority and agency and finding and exercising our voice? Are they the same?

- Consider journaling through your "whole truth." What is the story of your playing small and staying hidden? Tell Jesus your story and allow him to look at you, hear you and validate you.

Your Faith Has Healed You

"Daughter, your faith has healed you.
Go in peace and be freed from your suffering."

I'm positive this section will garner some resistance, so I will start with this:

The Good News of Jesus confirms that you are the Beloved, worthy of God moving toward you and sacrificing on your behalf. Do you believe this to be true?

Yes or No (Circle One)

Okay great. If you circled yes, please read on.[112]

Next question: The Good News of Jesus confirms that you are the Beloved, worthy of God moving toward you and sacrificing on your behalf. Do you believe that this is true *for you* specifically?

Yes or No (Circle One)

We spend a lot of time worried about whether or not a person's beliefs can check a box and line up with some sort of official statement, but then feel uncomfortable when their life *actually* reflects said belief (this is particularly true for women). Most of us, if we really believed the gospel, would have a much better quality of life—one marked by healthy confidence.

The faith that healed this woman was ultimately centered in a belief about God, sure. Of course. Without a doubt. She believed Jesus was capable of healing her. *But,* she wouldn't have been able to move toward that healing if she didn't also have faith in herself. She believed she was worthy of life, of dignity. She believed she was capable of moving toward what she needed. Her audacious actions reflected these beliefs. Without faith in herself, would she ever have experienced healing?

You matter. You really, *really* do. Jesus affirms this in the Bleeding Woman, and he affirms it in you too.

FOR REFLECTION:

- Jesus credits **her** faith with what has brought her healing. What would it look like for you to have complete trust or confidence in yourself and your faith?

- What would your "peace" or total harmony and well-being tangibly look like? How would your life change?

Collect Your Insights

Now go back and revisit all that you have journaled throughout this chapter. Pay attention to any patterns, themes of repeated words. What nuggets of gold can you dig up, illuminating who you are and where God is inviting you to Come Out of Hiding? Identify 1-3 next steps and write them down.

A Blessing For Coming Out of Hiding

As you end this chapter and your exploration of Jesus' invitation to Come Out of Hiding, I offer this beautiful poem by Carol Lynn Pearson as a blessing. Notice what words stick or stand out. Consider opening your palms, and reading these words out loud to yourself.

"Power"

> When she learned that
> She didn't have to plug into
> Someone or something
> Like a toaster into a wall
> When she learned that she
> Was a windmill and had only to
> Raise her arms
> To catch the universal whisper
> And turn
> Turn
> Turn
> She moved
> Oh, she moved
> And her dance was a marvel.[113]

Amen.

CHAPTER NINE

DON'T GO BACK TO SLEEP

REMAINING HUMAN-SIZED

The breeze at dawn has secrets to tell you.
Don't go back to sleep.
You must ask for what you really want.
Don't go back to sleep.
People are going back and forth
across the doorsill
where the two worlds touch.
The door is round and open.
Don't go back to sleep.

— Rumi[114]

IT's no coincidence that as I attempt to write this chapter, I'm watching Hallmark movies on repeat. It's the holiday season and streaming services have caught on to how women like to escape into perfect-ville. The storyline always has a way of tapping into desire without asking too much. Apparently, a perfect and meaningful life only requires a small town, a little belief in miracles, a cup of mom's special hot chocolate, and *a lot* of tacky Christmas decor. I'll admit—that would be nice.

If "Hallmark World" was real, I would be standing on the other side of your Wake Up, Stand Up, and Come Out of Hiding finish line, cup of cocoa in hand, welcoming you into a life of sweet bliss. With Beyoncé's "Run the World (Girls)" blasting in the background, I would say to you:

> "Look at you, powerful woman. You have conquered the world! Your courage and commitment to reclaim who God created you to be has righted all wrongs, smoothed out all edges, and opened all doors. All pain and suffering is behind you—now simply ride out this new life."

Maybe I'd even throw in a nice happily ever-after with your high school long-lost-love who's been trying to save the local struggling shop, if you're into that.

However, I regret to inform you, dear reader, that this is not how it works. There are no finish lines. Jesus' invitation into the female spiritual journey isn't a formula or a one-time fix-it plan. Choosing to embark on the journey of becoming most fully human—most fully who God created you to be—will wreck any visions you might have of a nice and tidy life.

Have you ever considered what *realistically* came next for the Bleeding Woman? After twelve years of suffering and dehumanization, she boldly came out of hiding, disrupted the system, and took Jesus's power without permission. It was an audacious act of liberation, and although she received her physical healing and a reclaimed sense of dignity, her story didn't end there. What was it like for her to face the crowd? Sure, there may have been some who were stirred by what they saw, and filled with compassion as they witnessed Jesus' actions, but what about those who couldn't get over the fact that this dangerous rule-breaker just disrupted their entire worldview? She may have left one label behind (Unclean), but I guarantee she picked up others in the process (Bossy,

Pushy, Hysterical, Agitated, Angry, Irreverent Woman). Quotes like "Well-behaved women rarely make history" make for cheeky bumper stickers, but the actual, lived experience of it all isn't so glamourous. *This shit is harder than hard.*

I don't mean to talk you out of Waking Up, Standing Up, and Coming Out of Hiding. The truth is, there is a cost either way: a cost to keeping the status quo, and a cost to disrupting it. A cost to staying asleep, and waking up. Ultimately, like the Bleeding Woman, you must decide that you want more. That you are more. And that who you are matters in and for the world.

A few years ago, I was invited by some respected mentors—my therapist and a local seasoned pastor—to a session they titled "Patriarchy: Ain't Got Time for That." There were a small group of us in attendance, all current or former pastors. It was a day-long retreat of sorts, using the outdoors to help us consider how we interact with patriarchy in our contexts, and most powerfully, ushering us into our grief from these realities. I showed up to this time a bit beat up. I had been feeling the rub for a while—the one that came from my full self not fitting in the space I found myself in. I was exhausted. It takes a great deal of energy to keep convincing yourself that something will ultimately work out when your body already knows better.

It wasn't until I sat near the grief garden—a little plot of land cultivated from the tragic loss of another woman—that I tapped into my sadness. For the first time, instead of making excuses or creating plans to bring necessary change (convincing myself I actually had the power to do so), I simply sat with my disappointment and missed expectations. I admitted to myself that what once felt like a dream filled with so much possibility, had turned out to be something more like a nightmare, and I wept for this loss. Tapping into my grief allowed me to honestly name my reality, and admit my desire for more. Admitting my desire for more opened up a new way of imagining my future, and *how* I would get there.

One of the exercises we participated in asked us to consider "our way" in response to patriarchy. We had an expanse of land on which to wander, and the freedom to explore how we would get from one end to the other. The symbolism was rich. Would I attempt to go through the middle, the most logical, well-worn, patriarchal way? Or would I find another route? My therapist and the seasoned pastor guiding the exercise taught us an important lesson about our God-given authority and agency that day. Sometimes, instead of staying and attempting to repave the path, smoothing out the bumps, and filling in the holes, it's time to create a new one.

During this exercise was the first time I gave myself permission to consider stepping out of my job as a pastor—creating a new path for myself—and as I did, a sensation of immense relief swept through my body. It was as if my embodied knowing wrapped her loving arms around my False Self (who had been hustling endlessly to hold myself together in a situation where it was becoming increasingly difficult to do so), welcoming her into the next chapter of my life. *"Yes, Bekah. It's time."*

And so, I set out to find my way to the other side. Now before this all starts sounding potentially inspiring, let me just warn you that making the decision that day to go my own Bekah-sized-way initiated one of the most excruciating experiences of my life. In the end, the grief I started to feel in the garden not only propelled me toward my full humanity but also stuck uncomfortably close as I continued to find my way.

Choosing to be exactly human-sized meant disrupting the system. Admitting that the space did not and could not fit all of me, by default, shined a light on its flaws. When a system depends on your compliance, it will balk at your agency. I was quickly labeled untrustworthy, and my character was questioned. It was said that I did not want the best for the organization.

Ouch is an understatement.

I often go back to the sensation of relief that day because it reminds me of my body's wisdom—that although the cost of getting out was higher than I could have ever imagined, the cost of staying in was even higher. There was no Bekah-sized way for me to stay, and so I didn't. Even with all the pain and loss, I chose my full humanity.

There are no guarantees on this journey, *but there is wisdom.* As we embark on, and then choose to continue down this path of becoming fully human, what reminders will we need, what temptations will we encounter, and what pitfalls must we avoid? I may not have a cup of hot cocoa to hand you, but I am figuratively holding out my hand. I see you and I know—*like I really know*—how much this is going to ask of you, and what potential pain it might cause. I urge you, though: please stay awake.

The Temptation To Fall Back Asleep

I was once teaching on the female spiritual journey at a small church where interaction and dialogue are the norm during the sermon. As we discussed the journey of ascent for women, a man raised his hand and offered a concern. "What if women become power hungry?"

This, of course, is not a male-specific temptation, just a more male-available one. He had a point, and we talked about the need for both men and women to not make the mistake of the other: men beware of thinking that the journey of descent means you must become something less than human, and women beware of thinking that the journey of ascent means becoming something more than human.

Truthfully though, I'm not all that concerned about women abusing the invitation to rise up. I'm not saying it can't happen—just that we are still a long way off from women collectively having the kind of power that needs to be addressed as an unhealthy matriarchy. Old patterns die hard, and what will be more of a stumbling block on the female spiritual journey is the temptation to fall back asleep. No matter how empowering an invitation like Wake Up, Stand Up, and Come Out of Hiding might sound, it is only a matter of time before you will question everything—whether waking up was the right decision, if you want to fall back asleep, and what to do with all the knowledge you find yourself coming into. Some of the resistance you will encounter will come as no surprise, but one obstacle in particular will sneak up on you and will likely prove to be your greatest adversary: *You.*

This is why the work of knowing and naming who you are and becoming familiar with your inner dialogue is so important. When things get tough, your False Self might go into hyperdrive believing it needs to as a matter of survival. And, at times *it will* feel like it's a matter of survival. Your False Self might tell you it's easier to go back, to fall asleep, than to continue. You will need your well-developed and practiced Nurturing Parent to show up and remind you that you are good, loved, and worthy, and that you *will* be okay. If you are not in your own corner, advocating for your humanity, it won't matter if anyone else is.

I encourage you to come back as often as possible to your sub-personalities—your Wild Child, Wounded Child, False Self, and Nurturing Parent. I recently participated in an intensive with a therapist and brought along my laminated circles, each with its own image and name. These gave us a powerful visual to work with and created a way to bring my already established inner work into our time as we dove into new territory together.

Several other culprits will tempt you to drift back into dreamland. A lack of community, absent self-care rhythms, and unchecked cynicism will swiftly take you out of the game. Be careful not to rush your process. Your body will inform you of the timing; your job is to listen. Sometimes your eyes will grow heavy because Waking Up means increasingly seeing patriarchy everywhere. A past participant of Girl Stand Up put it this way:

Sometimes the realization and awareness about how deeply entrenched the patriarchy is in each facet of life—from the education system, to healthcare, to politics, to daily minuscule interactions becomes devastating. This is where I feel resistance, or maybe exhaustion is a different way of putting it, on this journey. To wake up each day and quiet the despairing lie that no change can come and instead choose to trust this journey of awakening.

Give yourself the gift of rest. Make time for what brings you joy. Get outside and into your body. Have fun, laugh, and get into some good trouble. Allow your Wild Child to show you the way. Sometimes you might need to watch a Hallmark holiday movie or two, but let it be a respite and not a release. Resist the temptation to endlessly escape and be especially careful not to hand your agency over to doom scrolling. Take a break from the news when you need to. As my husband likes to ask his coaching clients, "How are you complicit in the conditions you say you don't want?"[115] Cultivate the kind of conditions and life that won't easily lull you back to sleep.

The Temptation to Hand Over God

The journey of faith that coincides with a female awakening is not for the faint of heart. As I reflect on the last decade or so, I notice how God and I have traversed a vast terrain. At times God has felt like a close companion, and other times, despairingly distant. My working God-image has shifted—sometimes male, sometimes female, often gender-neutral, and every once in a while, simply Spirit or Fire or Life (all biblical images, by the way). My relationship with Jesus has been particularly disorienting at times. I have needed to give myself permission to ask hard questions about his maleness, and to re-establish the contours and dynamics of our relationship as I move out of knowing him from the vantage point of a "cultural daughter." I still have more questions than answers, but my certainty has grown in my experience of God as a good and expansive container. No amount of doubt, disorientation, disappointment—or even disdain—can push us outside the parameters of God's love.

In some seasons, I've found solace in church. In others, that very same place has felt like a stranger, or more accurately, I have felt like a stranger within it. Asking and exploring "Who am I?" will always beg a bigger question: "*Whose* am I?" In other words, *Where do I belong?* Unfortunately, the church has a well-earned reputation for being not-so-female-friendly.

Most church spaces (both conservative *and* progressive) don't have a category for the unique female spiritual journey. When a woman begins this path she is often met with fear, resistance, and even rejection. Women are seemingly faced with a choice: stay and suppress the self, or go and say goodbye to God. Recent research is revealing what choices they overwhelmingly make. Women are leaving the church in unprecedented numbers.[116] It pains me that the price for full humanity is an almost inevitable exit from church. And it's deeply disconcerting that the burden to resolve this tends to lay on the women who leave rather than on the church.

The truth is that most women aren't leaving the faith when they leave the church. Our spirituality remains intact, as does our longing for God. We are resourceful and scrappy and go searching for what we need. The problem is that when you begin the hunt for spaces and content friendly toward exploring the female journey, you very quickly step outside the Christian world. There is nothing inherently wrong with this or these spaces. I can attest to the amount of wisdom and goodness out there (that Christian spaces ought to be learning from). I mean, shoot, even St. Augustine believed that "All truth is God's truth."

But there's a problem with this. When we step outside of the

Christian spaces we have known, we might begin to believe the message of those we are leaving behind: the Christian God is limited, not like us, and *definitely* not for us. Slowly, we acquiesce. We take them at their word, and we hand God over, as if they have ownership of the God of the Bible. In doing so, we reinforce some sort of man-made hierarchy that believes those at the top hold all the power. It may be empowering (and your necessary next step) to walk away, but do not be deceived. If in your walking away you hand God over to them, you are still giving away a piece of your authority. *Don't give away what is rightfully yours.*

I don't mean to make light of the disorienting reality many women (and others) face as they step away from religious communities and affiliations. I no longer officially serve as a pastor, but I increasingly find myself pastoring women who have exited the church. Our conversations often revolve around how to sift through and allow the good, true, and beautiful parts of their faith to remain, while discerning what junk needs to be thrown out. And these days, there's a lot to throw out.

If you find yourself in a season of sifting, I implore you to remember this: the God of the universe lives in you, looks like you, loves you, desires connection with you, *and* uniquely designed you to represent the Divine in the world. You may not be able to control how someone else stewards this immense privilege, but you can control how you choose to.

It *is* possible to say, "good riddance" without having to say, "God riddance."

The Pitfall of Immaturity

I'll turn 45 this year, which means I have a smidge of experience in this phase called midlife. As I observe my own life and stirrings, and as I play witness to those around me, I notice a reality that we need to be talking about sooner. If we ignore early waking moments and continue to suppress and keep our Wild Child in hiding, she will likely find a way out eventually. And if she is show-ing up without the guidance of a well-developed and practiced Nurturing Parent, there's a good chance she will *blow up your life.*

Although you may have (your age here) amount of years and life experience under your belt, your Wild Child remains very young. As mentioned in Chapter Three, our sub-personalities and the messages that motivated them to develop all came about in our earliest years. Your Wild Child is probably a toddler.

Consider for a moment what it's like to be with a toddler. Fun. Cute. *Exhausting.* A toddler does not have the ability, nor the desire, to give herself safe boundaries. Simultaneously, a toddler is never reserved about naming what she wants. She needs an attentive and caring adult to constantly be considering what she needs and what potential harm any given situation might cause if not proactive. She may throw temper tantrums. She may wear you down. But at no point does it become appropriate to leave her to her own devices. Otherwise, you end up with a toddler who has covered herself, her baby brother, and the living room walls with permanent marker. *Or something worse.*

In the past, we outsourced this parental authority to others—whoever our False Self deemed appropriate and necessary—to keep our False Self functioning and successful in her mission. As we begin to intentionally interact with and invite our Wild Child back to the table, we will need our Nurturing Parent (remember this is our only truly adult-developed part) to tap into our own God-given authority as she guides our Wild Child to safely emerge. It can be especially helpful to have a trained guide (like a therapist) accompany us in this process. Just remember that a trusted guide should always point you back to your inner expert, or God-given authority and agency.

The truth is some pieces of our lives need to change. Some of our relationships and roles need to end, and entering into the female spiritual journey will force us to confront these realities. But trust me when I say this: if you have the choice, initiate early and navigate that change wisely. Change is hard. Your life blowing up in an unhealthy way is much harder and inevitably causes unnecessary pain and trauma not only for you but for everyone in your orbit. If your Wild Child shows up without the wise guidance of your more mature and experienced Self, she might just wreak unnecessary havoc on your life.

Possible Pitfalls of Male/Female Partnership

One of my favorite things I do for work is tag-team facilitate a vocational discernment process for couples with my husband, Chad. In this three-day process, we guide the couple toward developing a unified plan that aligns and affirms each partner's uniqueness. Doing this inevitably brings up conversation around areas of misalignment, and what tends to get in the way of a fruitful partnership that successfully honors each partner as fully human. Because of who we are and our network, many of our clients have been Christian (or post-Christian), heterosexual couples in midlife.

It's not uncommon for the narrative to go something like, "For the first X years of our marriage, our 'shared vision' revolved primarily around the man's work. That seemed to be fine for a time, but is no longer working and we need help navigating bringing two people's aspirations into a unified vision." First of all, I just want to give props to the couples who are facing, naming, and then choosing to navigate this reality to cultivate healthy and fulfilling marriages.

It's been insightful for my husband and me, as we work with these couples (and as we navigate our partnership), to see the unique male and female spiritual journeys on display. If you need a refresher, here again is the diagram shown in Chapter One and Chapter Five:

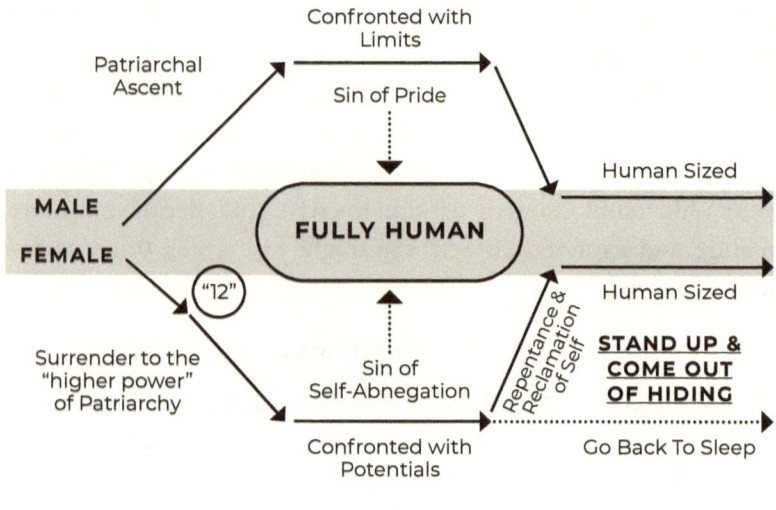

WAKE UP

After a time of the partnership centering the male's journey—supporting and often making accommodations for his ascent—things begin to shift, usually for the female partner. The couple has grown used to movement and momentum in a particular direction but is now being summoned into the next phase of their spiritual journey. The man is given the gift of discovering his limits and all he will never be; the woman, her potential and all she has yet to step into. If they (and it only takes one) choose to accept and heed these invitations, new dynamics are introduced.

If only one partner makes this shift, you can imagine the inherent tension. But, even when both partners say yes, there are new and disorienting realities to deal with. Just as a man is beginning to contend with the journey of descent, grappling with the role of pride in his life, he begins to see his partner, the one who for years played small, begin a journey of ascent, grappling with the role of self-abnegation in hers. She may begin to assert herself in ways unrecognizable to him. Although his intentions may be good, he may judge her actions through a male filter. He will struggle to support her and encourage her journey, perhaps even feeling threatened by it. Just as the woman begins to ascend, she becomes viscerally aware of how it disrupts those she cares about and has built a life around. Suddenly she is haunted by her worst fears, "If I continue, those closest to me will see me as Bossy, Pushy, Hysterical, Agitated, Angry, Irreverent Woman. It's easier and better for everyone if I fall back asleep."

Although I'm describing romantic partnerships, everything here is applicable and transferable to male/female work partnerships as well. I had a boss once who, in the same season of lamenting his inadequacies (naming his grief around all he was discovering he would never be), labeled what he was seeing among females in the world as "an unhealthy uprising of women." Although he felt the freedom and necessity of going on his journey, he wasn't exactly creating a safe and welcoming environment for women to enter into theirs.

To make these partnerships work, whether romantic or professional, we will need a commitment not only to our full humanity, but also to the full humanity of our partner, whether romantic, work, or other. Men and women can support one another's journeys by allowing and expecting them to be different. It's a dance (ballroom genre, specifically), where we ultimately move in sync, but only by taking the opposite steps. Each partner must put in the work, paying attention to alignment, placement, and execution of movement. Those who hold power can support women by remembering that the systems we live and work in tend to be male-created, male-centered, and male-normed. It won't be enough to give lip service to the female journey without also re-examining and adjusting structures, procedures, and values where necessary (in the workplace and at home). Simply having a group of men acknowledge the issue and then decide what must be changed won't get you very far. Women's voices need to be included—*and hold weight*—in these conversations.

I was part of a leadership team that considered itself progressive and pro-women, but when issues were divided along gender lines, the men were incapable (unwilling?) of getting curious about deeply embedded bias and misogyny. Over time, the women on that team were labeled as difficult to work with, hysterical, not resilient enough, unhinged, too aggressive, agitated, angry, and projecting their wounds.[117] These were all messages that communicated, "you are getting too big, and we prefer you small." Eventually, every single woman on the leadership team stepped down and left the organization.[118]

For men and women to partner together, they will need an understanding of the unique male and female journeys, and choose to empathetically move toward supporting one another, both seeking to understand and believe the best in one another as they uncover their new beliefs and abilities. But this empathetic movement should never require a woman to tiptoe around a man's fragility that may arise when he is confronted with his limits.

Ladies, We Need Each Other

Finding and cultivating community with other women is so important. Let's be brutally honest: female friendship can be tricky. My friendship history contains just enough hurt to make me very cautious, and just enough abundant goodness to keep my hope alive. I know that many of us are still recovering relationally from all that has divided us over the last decade. To complicate things further, we may have lacked a sense of true belonging in church. It feels like a massive risk to not only pursue community but pursue a Christ-centered community that will hold space for the unique female journey.

I find myself navigating relational spaces hyper-aware of how I'm too Jesus-y for some, and too female empowerment-y for others. It's tempting to dumb down or shape-shift just enough to be palatable, to be acceptable. But this too is part of the process.

The invitation to Wake Up, Stand Up, and Come Out of Hiding, and the work to reclaim the self, moves us into a different kind of belonging. As we differentiate and individuate, trusting God's very good vision and handiwork in creating our unique design, we learn to first belong to ourselves. And as we do, the purpose of community shifts and expands. I no longer need the community to validate and secure my existence. Another woman's journey of becoming need not be my standard for comparison, nor a threat. When I give myself permission to author my own life in a way unique to me, I free up those around me to do the same.

Be encouraged, there *are* other women on this journey—women who are awake to the beautiful and terrifying truth that Life is asking for more *of* them. Women who look for a path that does not pit faithfulness to God against faithfulness to self, but instead understands them to be inextricably linked. Women who don't reject or leave behind God as a good Father, but rather enter into a fuller knowing of God as Mother, too. Women who don't try to replace one toxic reality (patriarchy) with another (matriarchy), and believe God for the healing that will come with the integration of the masculine and feminine. Women who believe so deeply in their made-in-the-image-of-god-ness, that they boldly bring themselves to the table, speak the truth, and ask for more.

May we be, and find, and commune with these women.

A Potentially Unsatisfying Denouement

At dinner last night, my friend Amanda introduced me to a new term, "denouement." A French word for the act of untying, it refers to the final part of a narrative, movie, or play in which the threads of the plot are untangled, and circumstances are explained or resolved cleanly. A Hallmark movie would not be a Hallmark movie without its very predictable denouement. From the minute we start watching these movies, we know exactly how it will end, and the feeling it will leave us with.

I've had some trepidation over how to finish this book. I want so badly to offer a denouement for the female spiritual journey, closing out with a sense of resolve. I wish I could reassure you that no matter how hard, uncomfortable, or unsettling this journey may be, that relief will come. I can only tell you this: there are no guarantees . . . *except one.*

Ironically, as I write this, an email lands in my inbox with the subject line, "A Gift and Guarantee." It's a daily meditation from Richard Rohr offering me some reassurance.[119]

In it he writes, "My 'I am' is merely a further breathing forth of the eternal and perfect 'I Am Who Am' of the Creator (Exodus 3:14). This 'beingness' precedes all doing. I am loved—or better, I am love—before I do anything right or wrong, worthy or unworthy."

This is the guarantee: *As surely as God is, you are.*

The female spiritual journey is ultimately about fully stepping into and confidently owning your "I am." Jesus affirms and invites your full humanity—all of who God created you to be—to Wake Up, Stand Up, and Come Out of Hiding. And so, you have the power to decide: who are you becoming on the journey of becoming you?

As surely as God is, you are.

Made in the image of the God of the universe,

You are loved.

You are love.

You are.

FOR FURTHER REFLECTION:

1. After finishing the chapter, take a few moments to be still and pay attention to what is stirring in you. What do you feel in your body? What emotions arise? Do you feel resistance of any kind? You don't need to solve anything. The invitation is to simply practice awareness and to begin listening to your own embodied knowing.

2. I hope *Permission To Matter* has invited you to explore and take steps in the female spiritual journey, but nothing about this material is meant to be tied up in a nice bow (I wish it could be!). How might you continue to listen to your life, name who you are, and locate yourself on the female spiritual journey? What are your most important 3-5 next steps? (Some examples might include the following: find a group of women to work through the group discussion guide with, revisit your journal entries in response to the questions, prompts, and exercises throughout the book, initiate a meeting with a trusted guide, etc.).

THE PEN IS IN YOUR HANDS

The moment we realize that our life is really in our own hands, that it is a spiritual summons to be honored, and that we deprive others by not bringing our more developed selves to share, then we realize permission is not something given - but something to be seized.

— James Hollis, PhD[120]

I believe that for those of us who finally live in times and places where women can risk being clear and authentically ourselves, it is both a privilege and a priority to speak our truths.

— Elizabeth Lesser[121]

I wish I knew more about the Dying Girl and Bleeding Woman. I'd like to know their names, their unique personalities, and especially what came next. *Who did they become?* But this not-knowing offers us a gift. It invites us into the story and compels us to answer these questions with our own lives.

In my version of the story, after these transformative experiences, Jesus symbolically hands both the girl and the woman a pen. It represents something that their culture had not granted them: the authority to author their lives. Jesus didn't stick around to write it for them. He trusted their ability to inhabit and offer who God had uniquely created them to be. The bigger God story being written was always meant to include their important and particular parts.

The bigger God story being written was always meant to include *your* important and particular parts.

If the church and world are going to tell a different and better story, women will need to courageously move into their full humanity, take up all the space that has been designated theirs from eternity, and write their stories. It's time for you to take ownership of your life and spiritual journey. No one else can do the work. The permission you seek—the authority you look for—already resides *in you*.

The pen is in your hand, as securely as your God-given authority and agency runs through your veins. What is *your* story waiting to be written—the one that can *only* be written by you?

A broken and imbalanced church and world desperately await.

GROUP DISCUSSION GUIDE

Introduction:
Permission to Matter

1. What are areas of your life where you are tempted to outsource your authority or look to others to give you permission?

2. What is your relationship to your own embodied knowing?

3. Can you recall any "waking moments" or times when God has invited you to see and step more fully into your full humanity?

4. Where are you, what are you doing, and/or who are you with when you have a sense that you matter?

5. In the faith context, have you felt like you mattered? Why or why not?

6. If you had to name who is currently writing your story, who would it be (Peter Patriarchy, yourself, others, etc.)?

GROUP DISCUSSION • **CHAPTER ONE**

A New Road Map:
Discovering the Female Spiritual Journey

1. How would you answer the question: "Who are you becoming on the journey of becoming you?"

2. The author states, "It's not a 'biblical given' that our starting place is bad." What were you taught about your human starting place? What messages were you given about being human and how do you think they have impacted you?

3. How do you think scarcity has impacted your relationships with other women?

4. How does an emphasis on pride as a primary sin impact women? How has it impacted you?

5. How would your life and relationship with God shift if you understood self-abnegation (the act of rejecting or renouncing the self) to be the primary sin you must contend with as a woman?

6. In what ways have women unknowingly given patriarchy a god-like status in their lives?

GROUP DISCUSSION • **CHAPTER TWO**

Fully Human:
Reclaiming Your God-given Authority and Agency

1. How would you describe your experience of church or other faith spaces? Have they humanized or dehumanized you? How so?

2. Growing up, what messages were you given about your body?

3. If the God of the universe makes their dwelling place in you, what does this mean for where authority exists and what your body is capable of knowing and discerning?

4. What kind of parameters (if any) have you been given in terms of women and what kinds of roles they are allowed to have?

5. What comes up in you when you consider the invitation to look lovingly at the self?

6. What are ways in which you notice Jesus modeling what it is to be fully human—emotional, embodied, vulnerable, etc.?

GROUP DISCUSSION • **CHAPTER THREE**

All of You:
Reclaiming Your Lost and Hidden Parts

1. How aware are you of your internal dialogue? If you are aware, how would you describe the tone? Is the voice in which you talk to yourself kind or harsh?

2. The work of exploring and identifying our sub-personalities takes time, but if you had to choose one image that represents your False Self, and the perception or image of yourself you feel most attached to, what is it? What is the image or perception of yourself that you want people to see? (i.e. I am right, strong, likable, funny, smart, etc.)

3. Describe the conditions in which your Wounded Child was developed. In other words, what was your life and home like in your earliest years?

4. What stirs in you when you consider your Wild Child? What excites and/or scares you about the potential of her emerging more fully?

5. What are some practical ways you can cultivate your Nurturing Parent? What kind of conversation does she need to have with your False Self to assume her position at the head of your table?

6. What is your experience with the Divine Feminine? Have you been in spaces that taught about God using biblical feminine imagery? What kind of resistance comes up when you consider God as feminine?

GROUP DISCUSSION • **CHAPTER FOUR**

Made in Her Image:
Reclaiming God and the Bible

1. How would you describe your relationship with the Bible in your current season of life?

2. Has your faith experience encouraged or discouraged your ability to know God through your Sensing, Feeling, and Imagination? Share about these experiences.

3. How might the church benefit from more embodied and feminine ways of knowing?

4. Pause, close your eyes, and imagine God's face looking at you. Take a moment to receive God's delight in you. God is genuinely glad to be with you. Afterward, share what God's face looked like in your imagination (there are no wrong answers here). Did you experience any resistance to this exercise?

5. If you had only ever heard God referred to as she/her (if this was the norm), how do you think this would have formed you? How might your relationship with God, yourself, and the world be different?

6. Can you identify parts of your "God as Father" image that are more like a patriarchal father than the One True God?

GROUP DISCUSSION • **CHAPTER FIVE**

The Story Within a Story:
The Dying Girl and Bleeding Woman

1. Read through the story of the Dying Girl and Bleeding Woman (found at the beginning of Chapter Five) together and then share what stands out to you.

2. The author asks, "What happens to a girl when the power, authority, and government in her world is not God-designed, but instead patriarchal? How does this inhibit her movement into adulthood?" How would you answer these questions?

3. How do you think the experience for an adolescent girl has changed over the years? Do you think it is improving? Why or why not?

4. The author states, "What we have actually denied is our very humanity, buying into a lie that it is our duty to be less than who we were created to be. *And this is sin.*" Do you agree that denying one's humanity is a sin? Why or why not?

5. If a woman is to "turn away from the god-like status she has given patriarchy and move in the direction of her full humanity, reflected in the One True God," what might this look like for you? What are some practical steps she might take?

6. How do you see privilege play out in one's ability to stay asleep? Based on who you uniquely are, what invitation and/or challenge does this truth offer you?

GROUP DISCUSSION • **CHAPTER SIX**

Wake Up:
You're Not Dead—Just Asleep

1. Practice Imaginative Prayer with Mark 5:21-24, 35-40 following the guide in the chapter. If you prefer, you can be guided by the author by going to **BekahStewart.com/imaginative-prayer**.

2. Share your journal reflections in response to the chapter themes. The author recommends spending time working through the chapter themes individually and then coming together as a group to share.

3. Share your 1-3 next steps with one another.

4. Did you notice any themes or invitations from the passage that weren't mentioned by the author?

GROUP DISCUSSION • **CHAPTER SEVEN**

Stand Up:
Taking Up Space

1. Practice Imaginative Prayer with Mark 5:38-43 following the guide in the chapter. If you prefer, you can be guided by the author by going to **BekahStewart.com/imaginative-prayer.**

2. Share your journal reflections in response to the chapter themes. The author recommends spending time working through the chapter themes individually and then coming together as a group to share.

3. Share your 1-3 next steps.

4. Did you notice any themes or invitations from the passage that weren't mentioned by the author?

GROUP DISCUSSION • **CHAPTER EIGHT**

Come Out of Hiding:
Disrupting the Status Quo

1. Practice Imaginative Prayer with Mark 5:24-34 following the guide in the chapter. If you prefer, you can be guided by the author by going to **BekahStewart.com/imaginative-prayer.**

2. Share your journal reflections in response to the chapter themes. The author recommends spending time working through the chapter themes individually and then coming together as a group to share.

3. Share your 1-3 next steps.

4. Did you notice any themes or invitations from the passage that weren't mentioned by the author?

GROUP DISCUSSION • **CHAPTER NINE**

Don't Go Back To Sleep:
Remaining Human-Sized

1. The author states, "There is a cost either way: a cost to keeping the status quo, and a cost to disrupting it." What are some of those costs for you in both keeping the status quo and disrupting it?

2. Where in your life are you being invited to stay and attempt to repave the path, and where are you being invited to create a new one?

3. The author states, "If you are not in your own corner, advocating for your humanity, it won't matter if anyone else is." What are tangible ways in which you already are, or can begin to, advocate for your humanity? What next steps do you need to take?

4. Are there ways in which you have handed over your authority to church or other faith spaces that you need to reclaim? What could that look like?

5. What stands out about the intersection of the male and female journey of descent and ascent, respectively, and the dynamics it may potentially create? Do you have any personal experience with this in romantic or work partnerships?

6. What do you see as the top three most important characteristics of female community—the kind that will encourage (literally, give courage to) women to Wake Up, Stand Up, and Come Out of Hiding? What is one step you can take toward cultivating these kinds of friendships?

WISDOM FROM WOMEN ON THE JOURNEY

Participants of Girl Stand Up: A Nine-Month Guided Passage for Women were asked to share learnings from their Wake Up, Stand Up, and Come Out of Hiding experience. Here's some of what they had to say:

What have you needed to remain human-sized?

"Varied perspectives speaking into my life—young & old, male & female, churched & un-churched. Peers and elders who are willing to witness & be a part of my full growth & unfolding, not just the convenient or palatable parts."

"I have kept a photo of my 3-year-old self either on my desk or tucked away in my current read as a bookmark. When I see it, I pause. I stare at that silly, joyful, innocent child, and sometimes I cry for her and mostly I pray for her. She reminds me to stay awake. I also revisit my self-care rhythms and make sure I am doing one small thing daily, and one bigger thing weekly that brings me joy, that are 100% for me."

"Reminding myself of the reasons why I am doing this work. It has been helpful for me to remember that being my fullest self is saving me from cynicism, bitterness, or regret for opportunities lost. I have needed safe spaces to process, safe relationships where I can 'try it on', and trust in myself that I know who I am and that things that might feel conflicting can be true (specifically for me, loving being a mom and loving my career)."

"Women's voices. I have relied on the strength of other women, both those I know personally and those I do not, telling their stories with honesty and vulnerability. Their courage gives me the courage to keep going and to continue honoring my needs, desires, and voice."

"Surrounding myself with wise humans, intentional rhythms, and most of all TIME have helped me on this journey of rediscovering and unpacking self. I mulled over the intentional questions and repeated practices for months and they slowly seeped deeply into the core of my being. I needed this work to occur over an extended time—a retreat style or binge level of this material and content would not have created lasting change."

"I think the most helpful thing is finding other women who also refused to just forfeit our spirituality and faith because the old form no longer fits us anymore. I feel like I need a constant reminder that it's ok to take up space!"

"It has helped me the most to review the material every so often. Not necessarily when I am in crisis, but during the tender moments . . . I am so easily reminded by just looking at the different parts I created (wild child, wounded child, etc.) and welcoming them back to my table where I can return to my true self. The other simple thing that I do frequently to continue to stay awake is to refer to God as: Mother, Spirit, Sophia, etc. This will immediately help me connect with the presence of Spirit within me."

"Being open and honest about my spiritual awakening journey with other women on a similar path has helped me to be aware of when I am slipping into smallness, or slipping into a state of losing my voice."

Where have you experienced resistance on this journey?

"Mostly myself—it is so much easier to stay asleep! I have to think of this work as an investment in my future self and my daughters. I want to model living fully myself to them so they can see it is possible. I want them to believe there is a world where they can live a life that is full and awake and that it might look really different from others—and that is good."

"I still feel inner resistance when it comes to implementing new spiritual practices since there is still patriarchal baggage associated with so much of my faith journey. I have been giving myself lots of grace to experience God in new, less structured ways, and to not force myself to be on any particular timeline."

"Coming awake has meant discerning and facing lies I have lived/believed. I often battle my own exhaustion and overwhelm. I also have come to see certain relationships that benefitted from me being asleep to myself."

"I am a Black Woman so it's always an arduous journey being both invisible and also standing out. There's always resistance and barely ever rest."

"The greatest resistance has been from my False Self & the patterns that have kept her safe and small for decades. My own understanding of who I am 'supposed' to be in the world versus who God actually creates me to be has created the most dissonance."

"I have felt resistance primarily from other women who don't appear to value self-discovery."

"Most of my resistance on this journey has come from within myself. I can begin to make small choices of co-dependence or smallness, and then a few decisions later realize I drifted from living from a fully intact and awake center, anchored in wonder and awe, with Christ."

"I still feel the constant draw to perfectionism, and it causes me to freeze. Figuring out how to rid myself of old ideas that I need to be perfect in order to be 'good' is a constant struggle."

Have there been any unexpected obstacles along the way?

"My mom was a major unexpected obstacle. We've always been close, but it was when I realized I grew up supporting her rather than the other way around, that I had to stop and evaluate our relationship. When I took that break to explore (with some therapeutic assistance), she pushed back in a big way. When I got to the point where I was able to ask her to do some therapy with me, she initially accepted and offered to help, but then withdrew and eventually pushed back. It took her 6 months, but we were finally able to start at the beginning of the year. It was tough and there was a lot of denial and resistance during some sessions, but we were able to persevere!"

"As much as I know it is the right and good thing to do, it is hard. I have a community that loves and supports me, and I know wants the best for me, but this work pushes up against even the most supportive of people. It's a new way of engaging with me that all of us are adjusting to. Through this process, I have been working to practice tenderness towards those around me who are trying, even though we have hit bumps along the way. The habits of patriarchy are deep in all of us and I want to demonstrate gratitude to those who are open and trying to find a different way."

"As a result of becoming more my true self, my circle of trust seems smaller than it has ever been, but in my current season of parenting, and especially parenting a kid with a trauma background, my energy and time are so limited. I want to maintain relationships where I can be fully awake and authentically me. Finding my voice has put strain on my marriage too; my voice rubs up against my partner's desire for peace and comfort. This has been a slow unfolding, and my prayer is still that our marriage can be a place where we are both fully awake and present to one another."

"Not everyone in my life sees my journey as a positive thing and it can be hard not to take on their doubt and trepidation. It is difficult that people who once saw me as 'wise' for toeing the line now see me as perhaps less spiritually stable or credible, as I voice my anger and make choices they wouldn't make."

"I think the biggest obstacle for me is remaining grounded in my confidence of how God made me. This means journaling daily, recognizing when my 'wild child' is being repressed, and valuing the gifts that make me uniquely me without apology or need of approval from others."

"Feeling like I'm stepping into a freer and more authentic version of who I am, and thinking I can communicate my experience with anyone, but coming up against a lot of judgment and pushback from women who aren't on the same journey."

"Untangling my wants, desires, and passions from gendered norms and expectations has been messier, more layered, and more disruptive than anticipated."

What would you want to tell a woman who is just dipping her toes into this journey?

"Welcome! You are not alone. It can feel scary to start to look at all the ways patriarchy has silenced you and held you back, and there will be things to grieve as you acknowledge aspects of your life that have gone unlived. Don't be afraid of your anger—it is a gift that will connect you to your power, which has been there all along. This anger can be channeled to take you out of silence and into action, which leads to self-honoring, self-respect, and ultimately, healing, so you can live the life you were meant to live."

"You are more loved than you could fathom. You are more secure than you could imagine, and God is not changing, evolving, or needing anything from you in order to maintain holiness and brilliance. There is space for you to consider the things mentioned in this book, and there is space for you to take hold of them or reject them. This is your journey. But, to know God intimately is to dig in, to ask big questions, and to wait. Go gently with yourself. You are a precious one, and God delights in you."

"To the woman who is just dipping her toe in I would say, 'I'm cheering you on. While you may think the deeper you get, the scarier the water is, it's quite the opposite. The water may look intimidating from the outside but inside there's an opportunity to become alive in a powerful way. Depth actually equates to opportunity; awakening to parts of yourself you were unaware existed or were forgotten. The more effort you put into submerging your whole body the more you will want to swim. Get Wet!'"

"If you have ever longed to know yourself more truly, this journey is a beautiful step. It won't be easy but know that it is brave to honor your discontent and to listen to that voice inside that is longing to come alive. That voice is you and that voice is the Spirit, both working together to live a full and beautiful life."

"Woman: After years of hearing and internalizing 'flesh is bad!' may you start to realize that your flesh with the power of the Spirit inside you is beautiful, tender, and powerful. May you drink it all in. May you be overwhelmed and so thankful for those women who have gone before you to pave the way. Just go all in, once your eyes are opened, there is no turning back. This journey has been singlehandedly the best thing to happen to me as a Christian woman."

"Keep going. There is no sense or reason to hurry your own unfolding along, but do keep going. And there may come a point when you can hardly remember or recognize the girl or young woman you once were. God loves all of those girls and women equally and had this beautiful, complex, and unique path laid out just for you because you are loved."

"Believe that this work is ultimately very good for you and the people around you. It will feel hard and selfish. It will be confusing and feel contradictory, but keep going in tenderness to yourself and those you are bringing on the journey with you."

"Be honest and vulnerable with yourself as you dive in. Get solid support. Follow your instincts—you have them, so connect to them—and journal if you're having trouble connecting. This is HARD work, but it's SO worth it!"

"It's uncomfortable and unfamiliar and there will be a lot of moments where you feel like you're losing yourself, but if you can hang in there and keep being curious, you become more 'yourself' than before."

"Trust yourself, your inner knowing because it comes from the deepest place within you and who God has created you to be."

"When you're ready, this process is a steady companion as you begin to rediscover who you are and who you want to be."

"Remember yourself. You are your top priority. Believe that this is true."

ACKNOWLEDGMENTS

Writing this book has been a labor of love, a work of passion, and a part of my own response to Jesus' invitation to Wake Up, Stand Up, and Come Out of Hiding. I could have never fulfilled this life-long dream without a lot of amazing and generous people. Thank you for trusting, affirming, and supporting what God has uniquely put in me.

Chad, for being my greatest advocate, a true partner, and my best friend. Thank you for being secure enough in who you are, that my journey as a woman has never been a threat to you. Cape and Fiona, I am so proud to be your mom and delighted in who you each are becoming. I enjoy and respect you both so much. For my parents who always encouraged me to pursue what I was passionate about—and especially for a mom who showed me what a woman is capable of. And I can't forget Rocky—the cutest little lap dog in the world.

For everyone who has been a part of the book process—Beth Graybill, Joy, and Amelia at Punchline Publishers, Cari Jenkins, Kelly Trotter who knew a book was in my future before I did, Shannon for the amazing cover artwork and the gift of collaboration, Erica Krysl, Dan Cummings and all my early readers and proofreaders: Bridget, Kim, Amanda, Alexa, Dominique, Karri Ellen, Wendy, Amy,

Anthea, Kevin, Dave, Matt, Will, Justin, Nathan, Ryan, Dale, Jared, Becky, Arielle, and Dawn.

For all the women of Girl Stand Up—Anthea, Megan, Ali, Kelsie, Elise, Suzy, Brandi, Lynsey, Dominique, Haley, Ashton, Carolyn, Sarah, Matty, Shannon, Amanda, Kristin, Jessie, Chloe, Tori, Betsy, Shayna, April, Renee, Kara, and Hilary Jane. Thank you for trusting me and offering your wisdom and insight—it's such a gift to include it here.

For Kristin, Jessie, Pamela, Lizzy, Mercy, and Amanda . . . and so many others who showed up for themselves, and for me and my family in a very tough season—moving toward us, advocating on our behalf and even making many costly decisions that brought about your own significant loss.

And finally, for my Artist's Way group—Shannon, Amanda, Haley, Leah, Dana & Karri Ellen. What divine timing to have intersected one another's lives! Being on this journey with you this year has been fresh wind in my sails. You each are a delight. Thanks for cheering me on.

NOTES

AUTHOR'S NOTE

1. To learn more about the vocational coaching and spiritual direction offerings I provide, please visit BekahStewart.com.

2. In other words, in the world of women, I have access to an astounding amount of power and privilege.

INTRODUCTION
Permission to Matter

3. Sue Monk Kidd, *The Dance of the Dissident Daughter: A Woman's Journey from Christian Tradition to the Sacred Feminine* (New York: HarperOne, 2016), 18.

4. Kidd, *The Dance of the Dissident Daughter*, 27.

5. I'll borrow from Beth Allison Barr's definition of patriarchy: "a general system that values men and their contributions more than it values women and their contributions." See Beth Allison Barr, *The Making of Biblical*

Womanhood: How the Subjugation of Women Became Gospel Truth (Grand Rapids: Brazos Press, 2021), 16. Barr also references historian Judith Bennett who describes patriarchy this way: "A society that promotes male authority and female submission." Barr, *The Making of Biblical Womanhood.*, 13.; I realize that one's ability to stay asleep correlates with their access to power and privilege. The same can be said for one's ability to fall back asleep if waking up is too uncomfortable.

CHAPTER ONE
A New Road Map

6. Maureen Murdock, *The Heroine's Journey: Woman's Quest for Wholeness* (Boulder: Shambhala, 2020), 3.

7. Danielle Shroyer, *Original Blessing: Putting Sin In Its Rightful Place* (Minneapolis: Fortress Press, 2016), xi.

8. Lisa Isherwood and Dorothea McEwan, *Introducing Feminist Theology*, 2nd ed. (Sheffield: Sheffield Academic Press, 2001), 60-61.

9. A nod to Taylor Swift and *The Eras Tour*, one of the most influential cultural events happening as I write this. Also, I am one of those women. And one more thing, I did not learn the history of these men's views about women in seminary. I had to do my own study to find that out.

10. Shroyer, *Original Blessing*, 28-29.

11. Henri Nouwen, *The Life of the Beloved: Spiritual Living in a Secular World* (Redwood City: PublishDrive, 2002), 43.

12. Borrowing heavily from Carl Jung. Richard Rohr, *Falling Upward: A Spirituality for the Two Halves of Life* (Hoboken: Jossey-Bass, 2011).

13. Which is interesting, because even Rohr insinuates in his book that it can be different for women and those marginalized. Additionally, he affirms much of what I am suggesting in this book in his audiobook *Men and Women: The Journey of Spiritual Transformation*. See Richard Rohr, *Men and Women: The Journey of Spiritual Transformation*, (Cincinnati: Franciscan Media: 2010).

14. Mary Daly, *Beyond God the Father: Toward a Philosophy of Women's Liberation* (Boston: Beacon Press, 1973).

15. Hess's book is yet another resource I had to learn about outside of the seminary context from another woman on her own journey of female awakening.; And let's be honest, mostly *white* male written and informed.

16. Carol Lakey Hess, *Caretakers of Our Common House: Women's Development in Communities of Faith* (Nashville: Abingdon Press, 1997), 34-35.

17. Quoted in Kidd, *The Dance of the Dissident Daughter*, 29.

18. My friend Kim points out the reality that to be a woman in the world often feels like we are being asked to be everything, all the time (be more!). I don't disagree with this. I would caveat this by saying that in a patriarchal world, women are most acceptable if they look good and are useful, but that it's really important that they manage being this way *without* rocking the boat. In other words, be these things, but remain small. Even the most beautiful, and most useful woman in the world—if she breaks the rules around playing small—will become unacceptable to much of the culture.

19. Parker J. Palmer, *Let Your Life Speak: Listening for the Voice of Vocation* (San Francisco: Jossey-Bass, 2000), 9-11.

CHAPTER TWO

Fully Human

20. Clarissa Pinkola Estés, *Women Who Run With the Wolves: Myths and Stories of the Wild Woman Archetype* (New York: Ballantine Books, 1992), 173.

21. Elise Loehnen, *On Our Best Behavior: The Seven Deadly Sins and the Price Women Pay to be Good* (New York: The Dial Press, 2023), xix.

22. Dallas Willard, *Reformation of the Heart: Putting on the Character of Christ*, (Colorado Springs: NavPress, 2002), 19.

23. By classic, I mean widely accepted. This is the definition I was taught in seminary when I received a Master's in Christian Formation and Soul Care from Denver Seminary.

24. Dallas Willard, *The Divine Conspiracy: Rediscovering Our Hidden Life in God* (New York: HarperCollins, 1997), 13-14.

25. Alain Quiamzade and Fanny Lalot, "Animalistic Dehumanisation as a Social Influence Strategy," *Frontiers in Psychology* (2011), doi: 10.3389/fpsyg.2022.999959

26. Much could be said about the rationale given at times for slavery, and the marginalization of people of color throughout history—a heinous part of our Christian heritage.

27. Lisa Isherwood and Dorothea McEwan, I*ntroducing Feminist Theology*, 2nd ed. (Sheffield: Sheffield Academic Press, 2001), 60-61.

28. Isherwood and McEwan, *Introducing Feminist Theology*, 60-61.

29. Generally speaking, a Complementarian viewpoint advocates for men and women to have different, but complementary roles and responsibilities, while an Egalitarian viewpoint advocates for gender equality and equal roles and responsibilities.

30. And yes, we could also thoughtfully ask the question, "What happens to a man who is taught this about a woman?" These are questions that need to be asked, but for the sake of this book's purpose, we will focus on women.

31. The Prayer of Examen was created by St Ignatius of Loyola. Learn more at https://www.ignatianspirituality.com/ignatian-prayer/the-examen/

32. "Latin definition for: vocatio, vocationis," Latin-Dictionary.net, Accessed February 2, 2025, https://latin-dictionary.net/definition/39030/vocatio-vocationis.

33. William C. Placher, ed. *Callings: Twenty Centuries Of Christian Wisdom On Vocation* (Grand Rapids: Wm. B Eerdmans Publishing Co., 2005), 7.

34. Placher, *Callings*, 8.

35. Os Guinness, *The Call: Finding And Fulfilling The Central Purpose Of Your Life* (Nashville: W Publishing Group, 1998), 39.

36. Guinness, *The Call*, 40.

37. Barr, *The Making of Biblical Womanhood*, 106.; "Books," Beth Allison Barr,

accessed March 16, 2025, https://www.bethallisonbarr.com/books/the-making-of-biblical-womanhood/.

38. Barr, *The Making of Biblical Womanhood*, 79.

39. Barr, *The Making of Biblical Womanhood*, 106.

40. Gordon T. Smith, *Courage and Calling: Embracing Your God-Given Potential* (Downers Grove: IVP Books, 2011), 47.

41. David G. Benner, *The Gift Of Being Yourself: The Sacred Call to Self-Discovery* (Downers Grove: InterVarsity Press, 2015), 16.

42. Hess, *Caretakers of Our Common House*, 37.

CHAPTER THREE
All of You

43. Estés, *Women Who Run with the Wolves*, 37.

44. Maureen Murdock, *The Heroine's Journey Workbook: A Map for Every Woman's Quest* (Boulder: Shambala, 2020), 2.

45. Kidd, *The Dance of the Dissident Daughter*, 18.

46. Bill Plotkin, *SoulCraft: Crossing into the Mysteries of Nature and Psyche* (Novato: New World Library, 2003), 91-95.

47. Murdock, *The Heroine's Journey*, 136-161.

48. Murdock, *The Heroine's Journey*, 142.

49. Kidd, *The Dance of the Dissident Daughter*, 28.

50. Kidd, *The Dance of the Dissident Daughter*, 53.

51. "The word Shekinah derives from the Hebrew root *shkn*, meaning 'to dwell.' The term was used by Jewish rabbis in the first or second century B.C.E. to indicate God's presence among the children of Israel—and the term was feminine in gender." Virginia Ramey Mollenkott, *The Divine Feminine: The Biblical Imagery of God as Female* (Eugene: WPF & Stock, 1984), 36.

52. Benner, *The Gift of Being Yourself*, 83.

53. Benner, *The Gift of Being Yourself*, 70, 72.

54. Bill Plotkin, *SoulCraft*, 93.

55. Bill Plotkin, *SoulCraft*, 93.

56. A helpful resource for me has been *7 Stories: A Guide for Your Spiritual Autobiography* by my friend Dave Meserve.

57. Benner, *The Gift of Being Yourself*, 69-82. The reflection questions come specifically from Chapter 5, "Unmasking Your False Self."

58. Bill Plotkin, *SoulCraft*, 92.

59. Martin Schmidt, "Individuation and the Self," The Society of Analytical Psychology, Accessed February 21, 2025, https://www.thesap.org.uk/articles-on-jungian-psychology-2/about-analysis-and-therapy/individuation/.

60. A Christian movement in the 1990s that emphasized abstinence, modesty for women, and traditional gender roles.

61. *True Love Waits* was a popular evangelical organization and campaign that offered a pledge for young people to sign, committing themselves to abstinence.

62. "Eroticism." Ester Perel, Accessed March 16, 2025, https://www.estherperel.com/focus-on-categories/eroticism

63. David G. Benner, *Soulful Spirituality: Becoming Fully Alive and Deeply Human* (Grand Rapids: Brazos Press, 2011), 84.

CHAPTER FOUR
Made in Her Image

64. Sadie F. Dingfelder, "Our Stories, Ourselves," *American Psychological Association* 42, no.1 (2011): 62, accessed March 17, 2025, https://www.apa.org/monitor/2011/01/stories.

65. Known as the Four Functions of Consciousness; Eligio Stephen Gallegos, Ph.D., *Animals of the Four Windows: Integrating Thinking, Sensing, Feeling and Imagery* (Velarde: Moon Bear Press, 1991).

66. Gallegos, *Animals of the Four Windows*, 8.

67. Gallegos, *Animals of the Four Windows*, 8.

68. Gallegos, *Animals of the Four Windows*, 9.

69. Bill Plotkin, *Wild Mind: A Field Guide To The Human Psyche* (Novato: New World Library, 2013), 110.

70. Gallegos, *Animals of the Four Windows*, 6.

71. Other examples of practices are Lectio Divina and The Prayer of Examen.

72. Philip Kosloski, "St. Ignatius' Powerful Advice On How to Begin Prayer," Pope's Worldwide Prayer Network, July 24, 2018, https://popesprayerusa. net/2018/07/24/st-ignatius-powerful-advice-begin-prayer/.

73. Jim Wilder, *Renovated: God, Dallas Willard & The Church That Transforms* (Colorado Springs: NavPress, 2020), 157.

74. Wilder, *Renovated*, 76.

75. Numbers 23:19 reads, "God is not human, that he should lie, not a human being, that he should change his mind. Does he speak and then not act? Does he promise and not fulfill; A resource to check out: *The Divine Feminine: The Biblical Imagery of God as Female* by Virginia Ramey Mollenkott.

76. Virginia Ann Froehle, R.S.M., *Called Into Her Presence: Praying With Feminine Images of God* (Notre Dame: Ave Maria Press, 1992), 19.

77. In case you are curious or worried, thankfully my biopsy came back clear, and a procedure was done to prevent future issues.

CHAPTER FIVE

The Story Within a Story

78. Matthew 9:18-26, Mark 5:21-43, and Luke 8:40-56.

79. John S. Kloppenborg, "Synoptic Problem," Oxford Bibliographies, last modified September 2010, https://www.oxfordbibliographies.com/display/document/obo-9780195393361/obo-9780195393361-0120.xml.

80. Bill Plotkin, *SoulCraft*, 30.

81. In "Bekah's Version," I retell the story using details primarily from Mark and Luke, and including study notes to fill in context and add some flair.

82. From the footnote on Mark 5:25-34, Kent Dobson, *NIV First-Century Study Bible* (Grand Rapids: Zondervan, 2014), 1256.

83. Kathy E. Ferguson "Patriarchy" in *Women's Studies Encyclopedia, Volume 2* (revised and expanded edition), ed. Helen Tierney (Wesport: Greenwood Press, 1999), 1048.

84. Andy Lee, "What Should We Know about the Number 12 in the Bible?" Bible Study Tools, December 21, 2023, https://www.biblestudytools.com/bible-study/topical-studies/what-should-we-know-number-12-in-the-bible.html.

85. Mary Pipher and Sara Pipher Gilliam, *Reviving Ophelia: Saving the Selves of Adolescent Girls* (New York: Riverhead Books, 2019), 56.

86. Pipher and Gilliam, *Reviving Ophelia*, 29.

87. See Lyn Mikel Brown and Carol Gilligan, *Meeting at the Crossroads: Women's Psychology and Girl's Development* (New York: Ballantine Books, 1992).

88. Kidd, *The Dance of the Dissident Daughter*, 29-30.

89. Quoted in Pipher and Gilliam, *Reviving Ophelia*, 7.

90. Richard Rohr, *Men and Women: The Journey of Spiritual Transformation*, Chapter 2.

91. Hess, *Caretakers of Our Common House*, 44.

92. Hess, *Caretakers of Our Common House*, 45.

CHAPTER SIX
Wake Up

93. Kidd, *The Dance of the Dissident Daughter*, 10.

94. The guide I'm referring to is by my friend, Dave Meserve: *7 Stories: A Guide for Your Spiritual Autobiography*.

95. See Chapter Three, "Table Dynamics: Who Sits at the Head?," page 59.

96. "Mourning: Hired Mourners," Bible Hub, Accessed February 4, 2025, https://biblehub.com/topical/naves/m/mourning--hired_mourners.htm.

97. "Mourning: Hired Mourners," Bible Hub, Accessed February 4, 2025, https://biblehub.com/topical/naves/m/mourning--hired_mourners.htm.

98. John O'Donahue, *To Bless The Space Between Us: A Book Of Blessings* (New York: Doubleday, 2008), 14.

CHAPTER SEVEN
Stand Up

99. Jan Richardson, *The Cure for Sorrow: A Book of Blessings for Times of Grief* (Orlando: Wanton Gospeller Press, 2020), 146.

100. Julia Cameron, *The Artist's Way: A Spiritual Path to Higher Creativity*, (New York: Penguin Putnam, 2002).

101. See Chapter Three, "Our Gift to Offer: Wounded Child and False Self," page 67.

102. Amanda Butler, M.S., "Individuation and the Unlived Life of the Parents," Jung Society of Utah, Accessed January 7, 2025, https://jungutah.org/blog/individuation-and-the-unlived-life-of-the-parents/.

103. Palmer, *Let Your Life Speak*, 30-31.

104. O'Donahue, *To Bless the Space Between Us*, 42.

CHAPTER EIGHT
Come Out of Hiding

105. Hess, *Caretakers of Our Common House*, 53.

106. Elizabeth Lesser, *Cassandra Speaks: When Women are the Storytellers, the Human Story Changes* (New York: HarperCollins, 2020), 248.

107. Rachel Held Evans, *A Year of Biblical Womanhood: How a Liberated Woman Found Herself Sitting on Her Roof, Covering Her Head, and Calling Her*

Husband "Master" (Nashville: Thomas Nelson, 2012).

108. Joshua Bote, "'Get in Good Trouble, Necessary Trouble': Rep. John Lewis in His Own Words," USA Today, July 18, 2020, https://www.usatoday.com/story/news/politics/2020/07/18/rep-john-lewis-most-memorable-quotes-get-good-trouble/5464148002/.

109. Palmer, *Let Your Life Speak*, 6.

110. Estés, *Women Who Run with the Wolves*, 90.

111. Cole Arthur Riley, *This Here Flesh: Spirituality, Liberation, and the Stories That Make Us* (New York: Convergent, 2023), 186.

112. If you circled no, I encourage you to read *Life of the Beloved: Spiritual Living in a Secular World* by Henri Nouwen (or really anything by Nouwen). If you adhere to a theology that believes God hates us, and won't be convinced otherwise—well, we will just have to agree to disagree.

113. Carol Lynn Pearson, *Finding Mother God: Poems To Heal The World*, (Layton: Gibbs Smith, 2020), 135.

CHAPTER NINE
Don't Go Back To Sleep

114. Rumi, *The Book of Love: Poems of Ecstasy and Longing*, trans. Coleman Barks (New York: HarperOne, 1995), 3-4.

115. Borrowed from *Jerry Colonna, Reboot: Leadership and the Art of Growing Up*, (New York: Harper Business, 2019), 30.

116. Daniel A. Cox and Kelsey Eyre Hammond, "Young Women Are Leaving Church in Unprecedented Numbers," Survey Center on American Life, April 4, 2024, https://www.americansurveycenter.org/newsletter/young-women-are-leaving-church-in-unprecedented-numbers/.

117. These were actual labels given to women, including me.

118. Anytime I'm around any group that proudly describes themselves as "progressive," especially Christian groups, I think of something my therapist

used to always say, "When you think you have arrived, be assured that this is a sign you have a huge blind spot."

119. Richard Rohr, "A Gift and Guarantee," *Center for Action and Contemplation*, December 17, 2024, https://email.cac.org/t/d-e-svjriy-tlkrhtdkud-yd/.

EPILOGUE
The Pen is in Your Hands

120. James Hollis, PhD, *Living An Examined Life: Wisdom for the Second Half of the Journey* (Boulder: Sounds True, 2018), 79.

121. Elizabeth Lesser, *Cassandra Speaks*, 249.

ABOUT THE ARTWORK

"Dear one, the sun rises as you rise."

I never begin a painting with a plan. For me, part of the joy-ride of becoming an artist is the freedom to create as inspiration flows. However, I do center my thoughts, prayers, and imagination around a theme before I begin.

As I sat down to create this piece for *Permission to Matter*, I thought about the women who would hold this book in their hands. I played loud music, danced, and let gratitude fill me—for my own journey of waking up, and for all the journeys that are yet to unfold. I chose a color palette that felt alive and vibrant, one that radiated hope.

Hope mattered to me because I knew that for many, the path ahead wouldn't be easy or smooth—but it would be worth it. My deepest wish is that when a reader reaches a moment of tension or discomfort, she can pause, close the book, and return to the cover. My heart hopes she will see the bright sun rising and feel its warmth in her bones. I want her to hear and know this truth:

"As I wake up and step toward my true self in God, a kind of rebirth is taking place—one that will radiate light for others to enjoy, and will even lead them to do the same."

36 x 36 in.

Acrylic, Oil, and Ink on Canvas

ABOUT THE ARTIST

In early 2023, inspired by the content in *Permission to Matter*, Shannon felt a quiet nudge to pick up watercolors and colored pencils. What began as simple sketches in the margins of her journal soon evolved into vibrant explorations of color, texture, and form. Slowly and unintentionally, her black-and-white inked pages gave way to floral sketches, color palettes, and drawings that spoke where words once did. Her kitchen corner transformed into a makeshift studio, overflowing with abstract compositions and floral paintings. In this process, she was awakening to an artist that very much already existed within her soul—one she had long overlooked, or was merely asleep.

As she painted, Shannon discovered that her creativity pulled her into deeper self-discovery and honest connection with God. In a pivotal moment, she heard in her spirit an affirmation: "She (the artist) is important." The artist inside her was being called to wake up, to have a voice, and to be known. At this moment, she gave herself permission to release this part of herself into the world, to create freely, and to make space for art in her life as a wife and mother.

In 2024, she founded **Shannon Allyne Art**. At its heart, Shannon Allyne Art exists to create a space where human emotion, spiritual connection, and storytelling intertwine in complete safety. For Shannon, art is not a solitary endeavor—it is an extension of community. She listens deeply, absorbs life's raw moments, and responds with paint. She also serves as a kind of *creativity midwife*, encouraging other women to birth their own artistic dreams.

Shannon Allyne Thomas lives in the foothills outside of Denver, Colorado, with her husband, Matt, and their four children. You can explore her work and writing at **www.shannonallyneart.com**

or follow her journey on Instagram at **@shannon.allyne.art**. For inquiries or to connect, email **hello@shannonallyneart.com**—she would love to hear from you.

ABOUT THE AUTHOR

Bekah Stewart is passionate about exploring—and helping others to explore—Parker Palmer's haunting question: "Is the life I am living the same as the life that wants to live in me?" She is a Spiritual Director, a (recovering) former Pastor, vocational coach, creator of Girl Stand Up: A 9-Month Guided Passage for Women, and co-creator of Fully Awake: An Immersive Learning Experience for Women in Altea, Spain. Bekah speaks at churches, conferences and retreats on topics related to spiritual formation, vocational discernment, and the female spiritual journey. A gifted communicator and guide, Bekah holds a Master of Arts in Soul Care and Christian Formation from Denver Seminary. Jesus' offering of life and more life is what gets her out of bed in the morning. She lives with her husband and two kids in Denver, Colorado. You can find her at **BekahStewart.com** and across social media **@bekahstewart**.

www.ingramcontent.com/pod-product-compliance
Lightning Source LLC
Chambersburg PA
CBHW021626120626
46545CB00002B/420